A Magnificently Ordinary Romance

Also by Celia Martínez

diary of a romantica, vol. 1: lovers forgotten
diary of a romantica, vol. 2: lovers remembered

a poetry collection

celia martínez

A Magnificently Ordinary Romance copyright © 2025 by Celia Martínez. All rights reserved. Printed in the United States of America. No part of this book may be used or reproduced in any manner whatsoever without written permission, except in the case of reprints in the context of reviews.

The authorised representative in the EEA is Simon and Schuster Netherlands BV, Herculesplein 96 3584 AA Utrecht, Netherlands. (info@simonandschuster.nl)

Andrews McMeel Publishing
a division of Andrews McMeel Universal
1130 Walnut Street, Kansas City, Missouri 64106

www.andrewsmcmeel.com

25 26 27 28 29 VEP 10 9 8 7 6 5 4

ISBN: 979-8-8816-0088-4

Library of Congress Control Number: 2024947753

Editor: Danys Mares
Art Director/Designer: Tiffany Meairs
Production Editor: Kayla Overbey
Production Manager: Chuck Harper

ATTENTION: SCHOOLS AND BUSINESSES
Andrews McMeel books are available at quantity discounts with bulk purchase for educational, business, or sales promotional use. For information, please email the Andrews McMeel Publishing Special Sales Department: sales@andrewsmcmeel.com.

you didn't need to be perfect
you needed only to be
everything you are
to make a poet out of me

WINTER *(then)*

i

not all secrets are bad
some people just can't be together
so you smirk at me from across the room
and move your baseball cap up to see me better

and your hidden grin holds a mischief
that is only my secret to know
in an elevator, you pretend to ask me a question
when really, you just don't want to see me go

but one day, we don't care
as you ask me to sit next to you
two packed lunches kiss between us
and words, we can exchange only a few

i get a message right after
that i dim my screen to read
"i think you've ruined lunches for me because
eating together daily isn't a want, but a need

i needed to see you,
and now i just want to go home
because you're a vacation in a person,
and now i'm just sitting at work alone"

and i'm hit with giddy excitement
mixed with horrible dread
thinking of all the destructive paths
where love has led

but a couple of days later,
on your only day off,
you ask me what i'm doing,
and i say, "reading, finally getting over a cough"

"how about we read together?
i'll pick you up in fifteen . . ."
then we end up at this café, and
i take a picture of the prettiest man i have ever seen

in the picture, you're reading
you underline a quote,
then i give you a poem
inspired by the annotation you wrote

we're sitting in front of each other
so your knees hug mine
if love was beneath a tightrope,
i'm walking on a very thin line,
and nobody knows, really,
ever imagines that it could be true
that your voice replays in my head like a podcast
where my favorite guest is always you

True Love

ii

if you've only ever lived in hell,
i'd become heaven for you
even if i had to build the staircase to get there,
i would do anything for you

if you've only ever known silence,
i'd be the crescendo that kisses you awake
i would be the endless supply of love
that reminds you it doesn't always just take

if you've met only sorrow,
i'd introduce you to great joy
if you've known only confusion,
i'd give only honesty for you to enjoy

because shadows hide hurt
but they don't take hurt away
it isn't always sunny,
but i will convince your light to stay

if you've only lived half-hearted,
i would revive the other half
using the same neural impulses
that changed my brain chemistry with your laugh

if you've known only loss,
i'd show you what there is to gain
because falling in love
isn't always one-sided or in vain

if you indulge in fearful thinking,
how about a taste of hope?
because happy endings for hopeless romantics
will always be my favorite trope

so, my darling angel,
my favorite star in the sky,
when you meet heaven, you'll think it's hell,
and you'll sit in your car and cry

but anything worth doing
is worth being afraid to do
i asked god what his favorite creation was,
and he gave me a picture of you

iii

i met this boy
who holds anxiety in his hands,
who bites his nails to forget about it
because he thinks nobody understands

he thinks nobody notices him,
but i notice the room is colder when he's not there
he thinks nobody would miss him,
but i know at least one person who would care

because i met this boy
who is more loved than he knows,
who thinks everybody leaves,
but the thought of him never goes

who, when he plays piano,
gets in his own little world
as if musical love notes
are the only way he can truly be heard

he says he usually doesn't play for people,
so i save the three-minute video he sends like a prize
i'm the first-place winner
with tears streaming from my eyes

i met this boy
who thinks his beauty is skin-deep
how could he believe that?
when his heart i safely want to keep,

who doesn't know parties are created
just so that he can be invited,
that when he walks into the room,
all the lamps are instantly lighted

what do you do when you meet a boy like that?
do you just let him go?
let him become a stranger?
is he better off being somebody else's to know?

because i met this boy
who holds a silent plea in his eyes
for someone to see him, despite
an emotionally numb disguise

it's what he's grown up knowing
as he smiles and he talks,
forces himself to be perfect—
the way he waves, the way he walks

the way people see him
doesn't hold grace for his past,
so he pretends to be sunshine
to escape the shadow that he's cast

so when i met this boy,
he didn't expect that to change
what do you do when you meet a boy
who considers being himself far too strange?

when nobody gave him patience,
when nobody thought he was worth the
  time,
what else can you do
except try to hug him with a rhyme?

iv

i think you're really pretty,
like christmas lights on a winter afternoon,
and i keep thinking i might love you,
but saying that out loud might be too soon
so instead i just think you're really pretty,
really funny, really smart
if the most famous gallery hung a picture of you,
it would outshine all the other art
that's what i would say, at least,
because i think you're really kind
it would be the most glorious of holidays
to spend even just a second in your mind
because i think you're really pretty
and your beauty is a fact
the softness of your cadence,
the way that you act
and i keep thinking you're really pretty
because i don't have the perfect words to say
you're the leaves in october,
and i'm just a thought of yours on holiday
but the idea of us is really pretty
that's what all my friends thought
i keep pretending my heart is guarded
but, in reality, in your sleeve it must be caught
i think i'd like it to stay there
because the sleeves of your sweater are warm
that's what i was thinking
when you gave it to me after the storm
my heart deserves somewhere safe like that,
like the look in your eyes
i think you're really pretty,
and i'm very bad at telling lies
i think you're really pretty,
like sunshine in rain
i think you're so pretty
i felt that after one glimpse into your brain
that's what i would say, at least,
or i guess i just did
because i don't want to exist in a world
where you're not aware of your beauty, god forbid

v

i pretend
that the book is more interesting than
him
that my luck is all spent
that all of this happened on some whim
like i wouldn't care if it was taken
like my thoughts just grew up wrong
like i don't have a self-sabotage bone
within me
that begs to be heard like a viral song
like i haven't written letters
like i don't have entries with his name
i believe that day, i do,
that i was wrong for taking all the blame
so when i look over,
and he looks at me back,
there's no way in hell
my heart exists just to lack
so when he tells me his plans
of moving somewhere far,
i force a smile the same way
wounded skin forces a scar
because i want to go with him
i say to hell with all my plans
i don't care what i wanted
i hope past me understands
when he speaks of the children we could
have
the life we could live
the parents we could be
for that, any past, any present, i would
gladly give
and i don't hesitate to love him
i don't know if for me that's unfair,
but when he tells me about his pain,
i hold what he has had to bear
maybe that's what love is
he falls back to sleep again
so i grab a post-it and
pour my love out with a pen

vi

being around you makes me nervous,
but if nerves were a pool,
i would high dive, belly flop,
embarrass myself trying to look cool
because you make my heart beat faster
you don't mean to, i know
but when i'm next to you,
why would i care to watch any stupid show
or read the book,
finish the sentence, look away?
if i could be next to you,
i would let my hyperventilation stay
because, with you, i feel nervous
but the kind of anxiety that turns to humor
i'm laughing at how ridiculous it was
that my greatest insecurity was being a "late bloomer"
you make me shy
in that way that makes you have to smile
like i can't look at you for too long
or my heart grows legs to sprint a mile
i'm smiling at you, i'm blushing
"you're so pretty, by the way,"
and i would feel pretty lucky
to remind you of that every day
being around you makes me jumpy
in a chaotic sort of calm
like if a heavy-metal rock band
covered a beautiful, ethereal psalm
you make me feel excited
maybe you could tell
because when your knee kisses mine,
i'm put under a spell
that starts with "oh god"
and ends with "please no more"
my hands cover my face
i've never been giddy like this before
so i push my leg closer
we're both sitting on the floor
challenging the limits of tension
until we can't take it anymore

vii

i have this pit in my stomach
whenever things start going well,
as if pain is around the corner
and everyone except me can tell

so i start preparing for it
"how bad could it be"
i catastrophize, romanticize,
and unconsciously wish the worst for me

if i prepare, it can't hurt me
if i prepare, i'll be fine
if i overthink, it won't hurt
when i'm ripped away from these dreams
of mine

when my crush doesn't like me
when i fail another test
how bad could it be
when my imagination is at its best?

and i hold those thoughts within me
like a water balloon slowly filling
how much is too much?
how much can i protect if i'm willing?

and in this messed-up way it makes me
feel better
when the truth comes to light
and the worst suddenly happens
because pain felt the second time doesn't
have quite the same bite

so, it's not healing, really,
it's just less painful overall
i have this pit in my stomach
but hey! i put it there after all

when things are going well,
i feel like something is about to change
and if it doesn't, i will change it
because peace to me feels strange

and i don't want it to, i promise
i promise that, i do
i just want the butterflies in my stomach,
not the pit when i look at you

so i push myself further
and further away
because there's no pit in my stomach
if the butterflies don't stay
and you don't shout, you don't argue,
you just sit there and wait,
"if your younger self was in the
room . . ."
i would apologize for being late

for digging this hole inside of me
to hold space for vicious thought
if you constantly eat the poison people
give to you,
eventually, your body rots

and i tried to protect you
"how bad could it get?"
but these are just the trauma responses
that a younger version of me had to set

but it's okay now, you're older
you're not ten, or fifteen,
and i didn't say it then, but
"you're the prettiest girl i've ever seen"

and i love you, and i thank you,
but i'm not eighteen or twenty-one
you've fought many battles,
but this internal one is done

because this pit in our stomach,
i fear, will consume us whole,
and you don't need to pair with a lover
to match the sunlight of your soul

so i stop preparing for it
things are going well
and they'll keep getting better—
that's the new thought in which i choose
to dwell

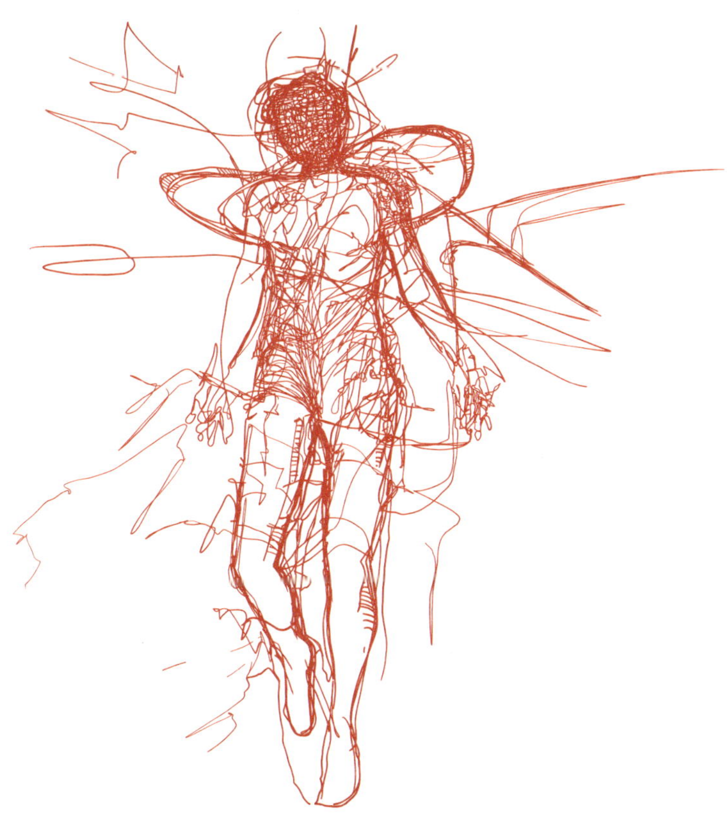

viii

if you could read my mind,
i don't think you'd ever be insecure again
you might not believe me, though,
so i'll voice these thoughts out loud for you, then
before i even knew you,
i only ever just saw your name,
we kept missing each other in hallways
you were just a blur to me, what a shame
so the first day that i really saw you,
i couldn't believe that you were real
i fast-walked away and shut the door
i told my friend, "don't make it a big deal"
my friend smiled as he shook his head
"i've never seen you like this before"
then we both burst out laughing
as i angrily shoved my safety goggles into a drawer
those stupid goggles
and the effect that they had
because i couldn't stop smiling the whole way home
when you texted, "i'm glad
. . . that i ran into you" "i liked seeing you today"
and so when i started feeling sick,
i prayed to heal some way
because i needed to see you again,
i wasn't gonna cancel that first date,
and part of me thought that i should,
but the rest of me believed in fate,
but i didn't really believe in it
if i'm being honest, you know, why lie?
i said, god definitely didn't put me on earth
just to meet up with some guy
then i see you walking,
you're coming up the stairs,
you have a gift in your hand,
our hearts playing musical chairs
with only one seat
and when the music stops playing,
our hearts crash into each other
"i'm sorry, what were you saying?"
you're the kind of beautiful
that handsome wishes it could be
attractive but the kind of charming
that makes a thesaurus out of me
and then you start talking
about the homes you've helped build,
the motorcycle in your driveway,
how you've always been strong-willed
and if my thoughts had legs,
they'd be in my mind running around,
desperate to find a tape recorder,
saving to memory your laugh's sound
that sound, your laugh
makes your eyes smile, by the way,
while you were looking at me
my angels were ferociously drawing away
your brown eyes, your crooked smile,
how your hair looks blonder in this light
paired with some big bushy brows
the eiffel tower begs to be such a sight
and the more i listen, the more i realize
you have no idea who you are
when the sun listens to the wrong people,
it spends its whole life believing it was always just a star
you are a star, you're famous
posters hang of you in my heart
my angels put the drawing of you between them,
and god couldn't tell you and them apart
you are a big deal
you might not believe that, but i immediately do
you made a writer out of me,
so i make poetry out of you

25

ix

you don't really speak spanish
i mean, not anymore
some past version hated
the you that existed before
he was a little kid with an accent
from two places, neither right
self-love was put in a boxing ring,
and there were too many demons for you
to fight,
but you wanted to be normal,
more like the kids at school
they didn't really speak spanish,
so being latino didn't seem very cool
you wanted to be admired
in a language everyone knew
until you met me,
and i recited poetry in spanish for you
"do you speak it?" i asked
i got a shrug and half a smile,
so i slowed down from my usual
speaking a million minutes per mile
"i used to," you say,
melancholic and thoughtful
"now when i speak my first language . . .
i probably sound pretty awful"
"can you understand it?" i ask
"yeah, most of my family still speaks"
you told me more in two hours
than most would ever say in weeks
i said, "to date me, you have to talk to
my parents"
honestly, it was kind of a joke
but maybe deep down,
some past curse within you broke
because then you wrote a promise into
google translate
and called my dad on the phone
in spanish, you told my family,
"*me aseguraré* that she doesn't fall
alone"
it brought you back into the boxing ring,
but you've trained for a fair fight,
and even though the demons hold more
weight,
this time you stop choosing flight

x

i loved you the fourth night i saw you,
when you picked me up at eight
roses in your hand
a broken cash register had made you late
i loved you before i knew it,
like my angels were on your side,
coordinating the surprise i never saw
coming
that stretched my heart far and wide
suddenly, it was nine
the restaurant was a little dim
they put us in a corner booth
our first date had happened on a whim
ten o'clock, the bar opens,
the bartender says hello
three free drinks later,
neither of us wanted to go
you tell me all these stories
about hardship and books
"you're such a beautiful pair,"
the kinder older man says as he looks
at the way you're admiring me,
holding my hand
we must've looked pretty great
because the man comes to a stand
"a drink for the pretty couple"
we both laugh but don't shake our heads
i think i loved you then,
but that's not where the feeling ends . . .
we weren't a couple then
i couldn't love you too soon,
so instead we walked around,
and i pointed out the moon
i pointed out your beauty
i pointed out your mind
you said you didn't want to be famous,
but your autograph, on my heart, had
already been signed
i started whispering it slowly
"i love you," i would say
maybe you noticed,
but maybe you didn't love me in that way

xi

i wonder if you dream about me
in the middle of the day,
if you play tennis with your thoughts
trying to figure out the best thing to say
the best way to say it,
if you should even say it at all
i think you should honestly just
pick up the phone and call
i wonder if you shake while dialing my number
i wonder if you hit send and throw your phone
i wonder if just the thought of me
makes you feel less alone
i think you should tell me that
if that is . . . what you think
i think you should tell me that sober
so i don't wonder if you've had too much to drink
i wonder if you would leave a voicemail
of all the things i need to hear
"i know i haven't said this to you before,
but i should've . . . my resolution this year . . .
is to be more honest
to be less afraid
i don't want to wonder
if i had told you . . . if you would've stayed"
i wonder if you dream about me
when you're fast asleep
i wonder if these stupid thoughts of mine
are ones you would want to keep
because i could tell you everything
the day that i fell,
i thought i woke up in heaven
since they have angels up there as well . . .
but i didn't; if i had,
god would've been so mad
would've said, *i put your dream person in front of you*
i thought you'd be more glad
i was, i am
i'm also back on earth,
which means that other people
have made me question what the hell i am worth
i'm sorry for that, really,
i didn't mean to do the same
i'm cautious of you when i know
you're not the one to blame
i'm shaking as i dial
i wish i didn't shake
i wish i didn't know about
how much love could take
how much i could give
how much i could lack
how long one broken heart
would actually take to unpack
it feels stupid, to be honest
feels embarrassing to have a crush
because we live in a generation
that romanticizes the rush
i don't want to rush with you
i want to put in the work to build
i want the future together,
the garden with roses we completely filled
i want to be afraid and do it anyway,
i'm sick of being tied to the past
i don't want to rush with you
because i want us to last
and if you ever wonder how i feel,
i hope you look to the sky,
ask god if i've ever fallen
"yes, but only you have made him fly"

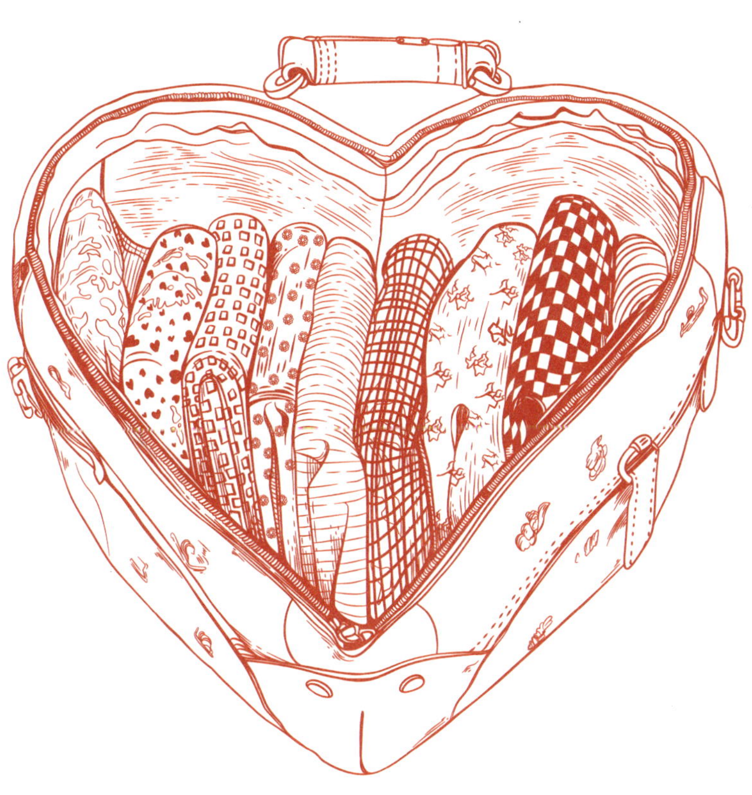

xii

i'm afraid that i won't love you correctly
afraid that, to you, all i'll ever be
is some untranslated, meaningless,
watered-down version of the best of me

i'm afraid i'll be okay with that,
afraid that i'll conform,
that i'll love you so much
that every day, i'll willingly perform

i'm afraid i won't love you correctly
because what is correct to me?
you know i used to look in the mirror
and hate what i would see

but i hate when people hurt me
i hate when i am used
i'm afraid i won't love you correctly
because i love myself confused

sometimes it makes sense,
sometimes it's all fine,
but sometimes self-care is more
than just a face mask and some wine

i'm trying every day
to be better than before
but i'm afraid that i will love you,
and then you won't love me anymore

because that is what i'm used to
not from an ex or some fling
it has nothing to do with other people
and what they would or would not bring

it's because i'm sitting at a table,
nobody else is in the room,
and i could just smile
and nobody would ever think to assume

that i am panicking
the table is half built
the dishes are all broken
the milk lays there spilt

outside, it's perfect
smiles and nods
inside, i'm tired of such
half-hearted facades

i'm afraid i won't love you correctly,
that i'll mess everything up
because if my dishes are all broken
why wouldn't i break us up?

why wouldn't i?
because the table will be built,
but the cracks will hold anxiety,
the chairs will hold guilt

the dishes are still served
everything will get better
i love myself
but to love you? i might never let her

it's terrifying to know that
what stands between me and fate
is some horrible belief
that i am the bad date

what if i am the bad girlfriend?
the bad partner? i must confide
i'm afraid to get into a relationship
and have it mirror what's inside

that's why i'm still single
i need to exude my own calm
i'm power washing my brain
i'm whispering kisses into my palm

i'm afraid i won't love you correctly
but not enough to not love at all
because fate is still fate
even if it's time you try to stall

xiii

i hope i'm the love interest in your story
the reason why you're a little late
the reason you took extra time to get ready
hope i'm single 'cause you haven't asked me out yet on another date
i hope i make you a little nervous
"what's the perfect thing to say?"
i hope you wake up in the morning
hoping that you'll see me throughout the day
i hope you check your phone frequently
hoping for a text back
and i hope that i then give you the security
to know that my responses will never lack
i hope you have a crush on me
the "up all night gushing to your friends"
i hope you're sending cute pictures of me
like, "my god, her beauty just never ends"
i hope you write about me,
hope your music has lyrics that spell out my name
i hope you scream to the universe,
"nobody will ever make me feel the same!"
i hope i'm the pretty girl,
the one you wish grew up next door
i hope i'm the second glance:
"they let angels into this store?"
i hope i'm the love interest,
the "too good to be true,"
the "just right, on time,"
the "my whole life, i've been waiting for you"
i hope i give you butterflies
the fear of messing up
the "can't take it for granted"
the "time to patch up my own cup"
i hope i'm the love interest,
the third chapter that will never end
i hope i'm your crush, your partner,
your very best friend
i hope i make you happy
i hope i become a psychological sigh
i hope the thought of losing me
makes you break down and cry
then i hope i'm the reason for your laughter
i hope i'm the passenger in your car
i hope the thought of me lingers,
even when i'm too far

xiv

my angels know the answer,
but they ask the question still
"does he know that you write about
him?"
"no, but he will"
"why do you hurt yourself doing this?"
"i can't help it sometimes"
"we call it a poetic reflex;
it's why we made your heart full of
rhymes"
"why is this happening?"
"you'll know the answer soon"
"does he know how i feel about him?"
"he knew that afternoon"
"i should let it go, right?
go and find someone better?"
the angels look at each other
"do you think we should tell her?"
"what should you tell me?"
"there's so much you don't know"
"okay, so start explaining"
"we will after the snow"
"why after the winter?"
"there's a reason we gifted you in july"
"born in the summer?"
"she knew the answer, first try"
"so you just want me here waiting?"
"no, we want you to live—
love is very beautiful,
but it's not the only thing you give
you give hope and laughter,
build cities on your own—
poetry and medicine—
you've never been alone
finding someone is magical
but even greater to find yourself,
and we've instilled in you the patience
to allow him to become himself"
"so this has all been some lesson?
you've been trying to get me to learn?"
"a lesson, yes, but not for you;
now it's his turn"

SPRING *(then)*

i

there's a certain kind of calm
that radiates from people who like the sky
who just sit down to appreciate it
until it makes them cry
who aren't burdened by worry
who aren't scared of what will be
who just lie down to focus on
the beautiful things that they can see
like mountains and valleys,
sunsets and trees,
who unlocked the source of happiness
without a man-made set of keys
but with calm, stillness,
a risk in wanting more,
there's a certain kind of calm
that i've never felt before
meeting you would make the sun jealous
the moon would wave goodbye
because there's a certain kind of beauty
in those who love appreciating the sky
dancing in the rain,
running in a field
where sunflowers all turn to look at you
so pretty, so healed
drinking hot tea in a garden,
reading peacefully by a lake
there's a certain kind of calm
that my anxiety could never take
time doesn't exist there,
the future isn't full of fear
maybe i'm irrational,
or maybe things have never been more clear
the sunrise is so understanding,
the waterfall so full of hope
maybe i'm irrational,
or maybe i found a new way to cope
so as i'm sitting watching the sunset,
there's a certain kind of calm
that comes only from your hand
and the way it kisses my palm

ii

dear future me,
i hope things are going well
i'm feeling pretty anxious
maybe you can tell
something in my writing,
in the way that i sound,
how i want to be running,
but i stay glued to the ground
i'm worried about you
or, i guess, about me
because there are all these options,
but i don't know which one to be
and that's just like us,
caught between two ambitious extremes
why have one when you can have
two life-changing dreams?
i'm still a romantic,
but love seems harder to find,
and if i'm not in love until i'm you,
maybe i don't really mind
i'm not the first version to say that
high school us was like that too,
and little miss valedictorian
even then knew
to believe in herself,
even if nobody else would,
and people got mad,
but her faith in me strongly stood
she's probably writing to me right now:
"does our life get any better?"
and just like you'll do with me,
i won't respond to her letter
if i tell her the future,
she won't understand the past
she'll wish her life away,
wishing for the time to pass fast
i don't want that for her
just like you don't want that for me,
and i know that my answers are
something to feel but not yet to see
so maybe i'm worried,
pretty damn scared,
because it's time to become you,
and i might be prepared

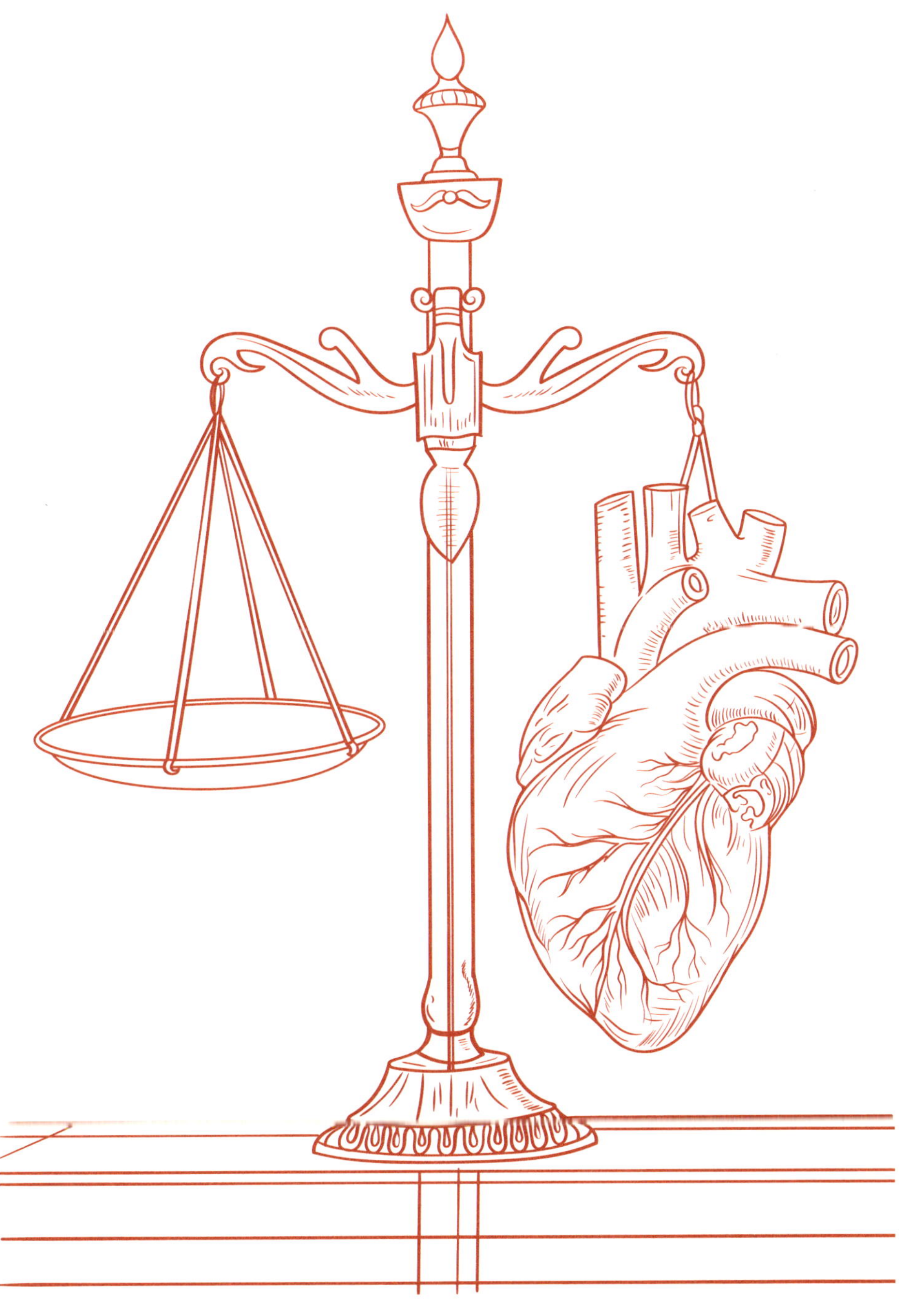

iii

i'll just be an example you bring up
to one of your new friends
"someday, you might love someone,
and you'll be the reason that it ends"

you won't specify the details,
won't ever mention my name
"someday you might lose someone,
and you'll be the only one to blame"

i'll just be an old address
your gps still sometimes reroutes to,
the name in a letter you never sent
that ends with "sometimes i still think
of you,"

an echo of a laugh,
a breath of fresh air
you'll put your jacket on
and find a strand of my hair

i'll just be a smile
stored deep in your brain
the first person you think of
when you see a girl reading on the train

i'll just be a chapter
of a story you'll keep writing
until you realize your favorite character
is basically me, just less exciting

i'll just be your favorite photo
that you showed everyone in the
beginning
as you kept repeating,
"isn't she beautiful" while you couldn't
stop grinning

i'll just be sunny
on the days when the sky cries
i'll just be the depth
that you saw hidden behind my eyes

i'll just be a question
you might never have an answer to
your favorite place on earth,
but you just barely saw the view

iv

i knew it, i saw it
there were two roads to take:
self-destruct forever
or find a new life to make
a new way to live,
a different way to breathe
because what's swept under the rug
starts to scream underneath
so i pulled the rug from under me
no comfort in the chaos to be found
the bullies made laughter
my least-favorite sound
and those thoughts come up again
like a bile taste while eating
they say, "that future you believe in?
i hope you never end up meeting"
but i shake that future's hand
"nice to meet you," i say,
and they lead me into a restaurant
that's lit up by the sun of may
two roads to take now
different from that first set:
allow other people to control me forever
or give time to the future that i've met
i don't know if i deserve it,
but deep down, i believe that i do
the questioning comes from
the fear of having something new
the fear of something better
that i alone created
their insecurities and mine—
i'm afraid they're all related,
and i'm tired of holding on
to beliefs that aren't mine
holding myself back
like my own personal stop sign
two roads to take now
but only one way ahead
allow them to destroy me
or finally fight for my own happiness
  instead

v

i like you
if to like was to love,
and if love had a ceiling,
i would shatter it from above
and then i'd fall
if "fall" meant for you i fell,
i'm perpetually falling,
and you never fell for me i can tell
or maybe you did,
but i'm too bloody and bruised
from not being caught
and just being used
you want to know how i feel?
i pull the pages with your name
pages and pages
that all say the same
you in cursive
you in bold
you found highlighted in all the words
i've never told
"i like you, okay!"
i'm frustrated that i do
because it's annoying to like someone
who might only be using you
"i can't be your friend
i can't even look you in the eye
because the expressions on my face
would never dare to lie"
i consider it for a moment
if i walked right up to you and said,
"do you ever need a vacation
from constantly living in my head?"
i like you, okay?
but i can't like you at all
because if to like is to love,
i don't want this to be how i fall

vi

if feelings were keys
what a melody to play
i'm sitting at a piano
because i see no other way

to tell you that i want to be bored with
you
i want to be stuck with all that you do
your poetry, your sweet singing
i could happily spend the rest of my life
with you

but i'm not brave enough to say that
so i let the feelings flow
when the world disappears,
you're my favorite place to go

i'm not worried; i'm in awe
you make the world love
if love had a ceiling
you're watching it from above

a gift to be admired
a necklace of red bows
hangs around your heart
wherever that present goes

for you i'd open every door
move you to the right side of the street
if we don't end up together,
i'll look for you in every woman that i
meet

and think of our first dinner
and the way your eyes shined
my knee next to yours
you're definitely one of a kind

they asked me who i'd marry
as a joke for some game
i threw my eyes to watch yours
i wondered if you still felt the same

too dangerous to tell you
too honest to be heard
so i play on the piano
like it's medicine and i'm cured

but i'm not,
so i play louder, but i start recording too,
i can't say how i feel
so i just save another video for you

vii

"forced proximity"
she says, "oh, what a trope"
because every time she sees him,
she's at the end of her rope
impatient and anxious
discomfort that consumes
looking both ways
before entering conference rooms
he sees her sitting there
as gorgeous as the first day,
but he messed up so terribly,
he doesn't know what to say
she sees him in her periphery,
as handsome as when they met,
but she doesn't turn to look
because she isn't over it yet
he thinks she hates him
maybe part of her does
but her mind flashes back
to how good everything was
he can't forget it,
and when the meeting suddenly ends,
he regrets ever telling her
"we'd be better off as friends"
that's the thing about feelings
they're rarely ever thought through
because if he had thought about this,
he wouldn't still be thinking of you
one day as she's walking,
he's forced to pass her by,
and every neuron in his brain
screams out an utterly desperate "why"
why don't you talk to her?
why don't you see?
why don't you let her know
who you really want to be?
something more to her
than avoidant glances
quietly ignored comments
she's given you way too many chances
something like the beginning
because it passed by too fast,
something to live in the present
instead of leaving each other in the past

viii

i'm writing our last chapter,
and i don't know how it ends,
but the one thing i do know
is that lovers don't end up as friends
i tie my hair up
with a pen tucked behind my head
looking at your last text message,
i throw our entire book across my bed
you know i'm good at writing
i could say exactly what i mean,
but i just stare at it for months,
wondering what unsaid words lie
  between
i don't know where we go from here
you know i said it as a joke
the "where are they now? not speaking"
the last time we ever spoke
i look back to my notes, wondering
what exactly happened there
i could end the story now,
but would you say that's unfair?
i close my eyes,
imagine myself in your brain
because what the hell are you even
  thinking,
driving me so incredibly insane?
i want to give it a happy ending
because i want that for me
but how can you end a story
that you never really got to see?
i want someone who talks to my family
and then brings me home,
not someone who says, "i want to be
  together,"
then leaves me alone
i haven't been able to write a new
  character
since you made our romance into a
  mystery
my favorite subject was always science,
but now i'm wasting time on our history

there's magic in madness,
all these things i've made
but why do i have to be courageous
when somebody else gets to be afraid?

ix

the definition of friendship
can be easily confused
with so many ways of thinking
hearts can be easily bruised
i can't speak for everyone,
and i never wish to be that way,
but my definition of friendship?
it's not just asking about someone's day
it's "do you want me to grab lunch for
you?"
it's "i'm proud of how much you've
grown"
it's "can we just cry together tonight?"
and "you can, but you don't have to do
this on your own"
it's giving great advice
"you might not want to hear this, but . . ."
it's a beautiful understanding
"you're always someone i miss"
it's not always talking,
but it's always speaking up
it's creating an abundant fountain
so you can both have an overflowing cup
it sticks around
on the days you can't breathe
people beg to be in love, but
i think friendship is more important to
me
it's happy tears
after doing something great
it's "i can't wait to tell you
i stood up for myself and didn't wait"
bellyaching laughs
handmade bracelets for the group
it's "i heard you were sick,
so here's the recipe for my favorite soup"
it's learned and rediscovered
it evolves every day
if love doesn't have friendship,
i would never choose to stay

x

healing your heart
will inevitably break mine
because i will spend years
pretending that everything is fine,
that i don't need more,
that i can always still give
i will spend years dying
just so that you can finally live
and you'll see it happening,
eyes grown dark on this train,
on the way to convincing myself
that love will always mean pain
love means saving
everybody but me
peace is somewhere still locked
because i have to earn the key,
right?
because that's how it's been
love meant confusion
nauseous from my head's spin
until i look up
on this train, i'm the conductor,
and a past version of me cries
because i still don't love her—
until today
i force the train to stop
all these beliefs i've been holding,
i force myself to finally drop
love doesn't mean healing
it's a generous side effect, it's true
because somebody unpacks their
baggage
to make space for loving you
maybe it's not meant to save you,
but it gives you a different smile
it memorizes your number
because you're the first person they
always dial
i hope, if peace is locked,
that there are abundant keys,
that love finds you everywhere
and gently implores, "take these"
i hope love means the kind of stillness
that always promotes growth,
and if love is a place with beautiful
opportunities,
i hope there's room for us both

xi

they say everyone you attract
is a reflection of yourself,
but the mirror must've been dirty,
must've collapsed on itself
if this is how i am,
i fear for my heart,
and if love is accountability,
it's time i acknowledge my most hated
part
these things that are broken
i have to put back together
i toss the umbrella, and i accept
my internal weather
i don't like this person
this person being me
or at least, in the past,
the person i would be
but a lot has changed
i'd like to think i've grown,
but i make bad decisions
when better, i should've known
or i make great decisions,
then overthink until i'm numb
i'd like to think i'm smart,
but i can act so dumb
if this is my reflection,
i can't just take the good,
and when they ask me to help them,
there's a reason why i would
because you were me
i was who i really wanted,
and every part of me that died
came back; i was haunted
unfinished business,
like really seeing myself

they say everyone you attract
is just a reflection of yourself
like the guy who bought two pizzas
because i couldn't decide my order
the one that caught me mid-fall
because i really wasn't a skateboarder
the one who lay next to me on a
hammock
just asking about my day
the one that sent a whole voice-recorded
poem
because he knew exactly what to say
maybe things haven't worked,
but they haven't been all bad
because some of the best parts of me
were parts that they had

xii

words were created
so the poets could write about your smile,
and i was never good at poetry,
so writing this took me a while
i played around with prose,
essays, and letters
nonfiction writing
gave worth to cruel doubters
undeserving of rhymes
that give compliments that seem like puzzles,
who made my heart feel
like one of my most worthless muscles
so when the walls came up,
i awoke once again
suddenly, i'm the dream woman,
too intimidating for nightmare men
writers with immortality
on the tips of their pens
write novels of us
describing how we're "just friends"
but what are relationships
if not two friends in love?
or, at least, that's what i hope
that's what i pray for from above
people get confused,
start to play with emotions,
as if breaking hearts was a company,
and they're desperate for promotions
well, if heartbreak is a job,
here's my letter of resignation
because i'm too stubborn to conform to
the romantic ideals of the new generation
because i think words were created
to write about your smile
to remind people that they feel like home
to appreciate a heart's unique style
and i would bring you back
the world needs people like you,
and words must have been created
so i could remind you that's true

I
M
S
O
R
R
Y

xiii

when a picture is taken,
how many words go unspoken?
our mutual friend sits in the middle,
like our hearts have never been broken
by each other or by others
who has the time to keep track?
do you ever sit there and wish
that the two of us could go back?
i don't think i do
a lot of things have changed,
but do you sit there and realize
you're the main reason we're estranged?
i still have the same friends
i told you they meant a lot to me,
and i meant it when i said
you could be my friend if you wanted to be

xiv

i care about you,
even if we never speak again
i care about you,
even if i say i can't be your friend
i care about your birthday,
even if i never send a note
in fact, i remember it so well,
i put it in the first book i ever wrote
i care about your future
i consider your heart
i hope your soulmate's kind
and they don't tear you apart
i care about you,
and this causes me a lot of pain
so i try to stop caring
to feel a little more sane
because i care about you in august,
when you move away for school,
but i care about my boundaries
respect was my one and only rule
i care about you in the cold,
when my hands feel like they're frozen
i care about you even when i wish
i'm the person you would have chosen
i care about you with angels
they cry on my shoulder
wishing and praying
we had met when we were older
but what would have changed?
would you have actually cared about me?
somewhere in the future,
would you have actually loved me?
i cared about you,
and maybe i care about you still,
but one day, someone will care enough
to stay,
and this time, they will

xv

i close the entrance,
but you put your foot in the door,
saying, “please, can we just
talk . . . a little more?”
i say, “there’s nothing to speak about
you just want your ego fed
i told you how i felt about you,
and it went straight to your head
i aimed it at your heart
but you must be made of armor
made of useless lines
to be called ‘quite the charmer’”
“i just want to be friends”
you don’t take a second to think about my feelings
i have climbed up from basements
while you’ve always lived on ceilings
i made my heart soft
through ruthless exertion
you ask for forgiveness
with gaslit assertion
disgusting behavior
it makes me feel sick
you try to compliment me,
but it just feels like another trick
feels like a game
that you want to keep playing
“just listen to me!”
but you don’t hear what i’m saying
i wanted it to happen
i hoped and prayed that it would
you said you couldn’t love me,
but i wished that you could
wished you’d feel better,
wished you’d return
wished and wished that you weren’t
just another lesson to learn

xvi

there's a version of me that didn't make it
she stayed sobbing under a table
she held the phone in her hand,
and i watched "empty" become her only label
i saw her lose interest
suddenly, nobody came to mind
when asked who cares about her,
she felt broken and behind
she tried to ask for help
from people she loved very dearly,
but they were always unavailable,
happier without her, clearly
that version of me didn't make it,
and i feel guilty every day
because, eventually, when i saved her,
her hope was lost to decay
there was something different about her
she didn't talk about it often,
like she carried pain on her shoulders,
but her heart could only soften
she kept to herself more then,
like she was afraid of disappearing,
like she kept singing songs
that everyone was sick of hearing
the house grew quiet then,
but at least she wasn't crying
however, inside, this version of me,
still remembered dying
still remembered the call
"you're so needy," he said,
but she just wanted company
an escape from inside her head,
but she couldn't really escape it,
so she stayed accepting the worst
unable to make a decision
maybe he would break up with her first . . .
eventually, he did
that version of me went too,
but one day she came back and said,
i'm glad i became you

xvii

i forgive you,
if only for my own mental sanity
i forgive you because of the way
i will always believe in humanity
you might not deserve it,
and i might never forget,
but i no longer want my emotions
to feel like a ticking threat
there's so much that i buried
i didn't even think that could be true
there's so many things i wish i'd said
it's time i say them to you
what a full circle
that's the way this life goes
i see you wave through the window
while i watch my door close
it's a little sad, isn't it?
but also kind of exciting
that my heart was open enough
to be so inviting
and yours was too,
some things you still save
a poem in a notebook
i hope it reminds you to be brave
important lessons to learn,
like making sure to take things slow,
like caring about people
is probably something to openly show
like miscommunication
can lead to a lot of pain,
like having strong feelings for
someone wasn't in vain
i forgive you because i like those
memories,
and, sure, maybe that's all they'll ever be
but most of all, i finally forgive you
because i really want to forgive me

xviii

there are a lot of things i wanted to say
then,
but i know how i can be,
"and if you could choose to be with
anyone,
why would you ever choose to be with
me?
i'm sorry, i mean, i'm not
i mean, i wish you couldn't tell
i'm sorry, i mean, i'm not
i mean, maybe for you, i fell
maybe i'm still falling"
but i don't say that; instead,
"i'm sorry, i mean, i'm not
i mean, what if i'm the book you wish
you never read?"
we're getting to the good part,
the climax of the scene
here are all the worst parts of me
and exactly what they mean
there are a lot of things i want to say
like, am i the door you regret having
budged?
here are all the worst parts of me
i'm ready to be judged
i'm sorry, i mean, i'm not
i mean, people have been mean
i'm sorry, i mean, i'm not
i mean, some scars can't be scrubbed
clean
i mean, i'm still cleaning
years in advance
i mean, people have hurt me
because i gave them the chance
there are a lot of things they said then
i'm plucking splinters from my heart
i mean, if you asked how they hurt me,
i wouldn't even know where to start
so if you could choose to be with anyone,
why would i assume it would be me with
you?
and even then, what if you're choosing
someone you later wish you never knew?

xix

there were a lot of things i wanted to say
then,
but i didn't know where to start
because you turn absolute train wrecks
into these poetic pieces of art

and i'm sitting watching it happen
letting all this time pass
i'm praying like a sinner
who's somehow leading the mass

if i could choose to be with anyone,
i'd save you for later
because i saw myself in the mirror
and said, "don't you dare date her"

because i'm sitting in a coffee shop
writing like i could be a poet too
thinking of the most meaningful ways
for me to apologize to you

writing about stars
and the way that they fall
if i were a telescope
i'd never see the rest of the sky at all

because i would keep my eyes on one
the star to outshine the rest
i can't write for shit
but i'm here trying my best

we're getting to the good part
the part where he begs
i didn't know that stars
could grow arms and legs

"please, i messed up
i was too scared to try
please don't think i meant it"
i let out a big sigh

text, edit,
write, don't send
here are the worst parts of me
that i don't know how to mend

there were a lot of things i wanted to say
but i kept typing just to delete
you were the open door
to a home where i should've taken a seat

you were the person
who i never should've let go
all the parts you hate about yourself
i was lucky to get to know

so if you could choose to be with anyone
i'd hope it'd be with me
i would choose you over and over
the star i'd forget the world to see

xx

in my attic, i have boxes
packages of words left unsaid
stories missing their ending
because i don't know where they would
have led
but the attic is overflowing
suddenly boxes fill my room
the kitchen, the counters,
my mind, they all consume
but then one day
the boxes begin to share aloud
that the memories include people
with whom they are sentimentally bound
some i reach out to
but not to begin again
i unpack the boxes
as i put down my pen
i hand out these gifts
no tears left in sight
all these words that i've written
at the time, they felt right
love letters about laughs
poems about third dates
novels that i wrote
as the person who eternally waits
some boxes i burn
i don't even dare to open
because i don't need to remember
the times i was most broken
slowly and kindly,
i tear the boxes down
bags suddenly empty,
i float where i used to drown
it's peaceful within me
i make space for something more,
and then the attic is empty
or, i guess, full of what i most adore

xxi

if you see a blinking cursor,
do you take it as an invitation to speak?
or if you see my three dots typing,
will you think i'm far too weak?
spoiler alert: i am weak,
or at least that's what people say,
if weak meant "full of strength"
yeah, i'm feeling pretty weak today
because it takes courage, to be honest,
to sit down with feelings,
to climb up flights of stairs
just for a chance to break ceilings
"love," what people know it as,
is called superficial and lazy
"love," what people feel it as,
is insanity, heart hazy
butterflies that wreak havoc
quickly turn to bitter moths
soft, silky sheets
are now the itchiest of cloths
"love," derogatory,
has many conflicting faces
but can't stand to be with me
can't commit to those spaces
but the spaces on my keyboard
don't hold any letters,
and the way that i love is like
the feeling of warmth without sweaters
peaceful and calm
honest and fair
hoping you're okay
if i see that you're not there
crochet hearts,
laughter full of feeling
the way that i love
makes you feel like you're healing
generous, understanding
i hear what you're saying
people always leave, but
i have a bad habit of staying
so today, i embrace silence
i write to myself instead
because the way that i love
has people saying romance isn't dead

xxii

you know i would do it all again
all the heartbreak and healing
thunderstorms of pain
just for the sunshine of feeling
the hesitancy as you move closer
the fear of messing up
everything could be ruined
and i would still order that *cafecito* cup
i would drink it slowly
recall all that has passed
i would do it all again,
but this time i wouldn't move so fast
a flame that burns quickly
will inevitably burn out
but it's been too long, and
you're still the one i write about
softly, quietly,
like i can't press the pen fully down
it would bleed to the other pages
i would see you around town,
but the ink suddenly spills
there you are on every page
in the play of my mind,
you never once leave the stage
there we are, happy,
together, not alone
there, my house is messy,
but you still come home
again and again
you decide to choose me
and oh, my decision,
how easy it would be
i'd speak so freely
abandon overthinking
teach my heart to swim
so for once it stops sinking
i would do it all again
just for a chance to see it through
because there are many people in the world,
but none of them compare to you

xxiii

maybe that's how it was meant to be
"strangers," they say,
like our angels weren't looking forward
to when we met, that day
i heard they kept countdowns
each circled the day and the year
they sat and looked out windows
they sighed and left a tear
then, out of nowhere
suddenly came a large sound
hinting at the place
where a lost soul could be found
souls, i should say
two halves of a whole,
and angels aren't thieves
but for you, my heart they suddenly stole
together, they conspired
they alerted the masses
they said, "love exists
pay attention! or it passes"
and it passed, one day
as i was sitting there reading
"strangers," they say,
like our angels weren't pleading
"please, just remember"
the wind started to sing
rain started pouring
as their eyes started to sting
my angel and yours
looked at each other, teary
my angel fell into your angel's arms,
both broken and weary
"please," the angel told you
"she's all i have left
i can't leave without her
my heart she has theft"
"remember, please,
before we were angels, we used to be you
we guard you in this life
please fall in love too"

xxiv

in another life, we're together
you have blurry pictures of me on your phone
documenting unconfined happiness
as ice cream drips from a waffle cone
in that life, we find each other younger
we start dating as we finish high school
we end up at the same college
and convince each other that we're "super cool"
we're not, of course,
but neither of us cares
we spend more time in truths
than entertaining ridiculous dares
we grow up together
two kids forced to be brave
little miss independent
is never a damsel to save
but there, we don't know absence
the heart fondness that grows
there we are two secrets that
nobody else ever really knows
maybe not a bad thing,
but i never meet my best friend
so many opportunities
i let go of and watch end
and there, i don't mind it
i'm happy with you still,
but i never learn of the dreams
that, in this life, i will
there i am an extension,
a part of your growth
there we are together
but not individuals us both
in another life, we're together
we get married by twenty-five,
but i never really learn
what it means to be alive
there i don't write
this version of me is gone
but i am still content
just sitting on our front lawn
but i never leave our town
i stay there an entire life
i never cry myself to sleep,
but i'm only ever just your wife
in another life, we're together
children, we have three
and they ask to know the story
of the person i never got to be

xxv

i deleted the list
you know that story well
i don't have to repeat
something you could easily tell
but i didn't need a list
to remember what you like
raisin bran cereal
riding on your motorbike
sourdough bread
tres leches cake
time to yourself
people who aren't fake
cada día que aprendía
más sobre ti
noté como parecías
un reflejo de mi
reading at bars
cafecito y mezcal
fried yucca with garlic
mojo con a little *sal*
slow, well-rested mornings
brunches turned to lunch
men never get flowers,
so i gave you your first bunch
red gatorade after a workout
sitting doing nothing
you hate "too chocolaty"
but love a good banana muffin
cinnamon chai lattes
you turned twenty-four today
mr. too quiet
sometimes doesn't know what to say
making cars dance,
screaming, "tonight, we are young"
some books might be written,
but some stories still aren't done

there was no need for fall
when for you i already fell
some of the best-kept secrets
i learned, only poetry can tell

SUMMER *(then)*

i

it's raining in the city
i'm driving a vehicle i no longer know,
and i've never felt comfortable
driving in cars alone
it reminds me of risk
that bravery has great reward
but what if i reach the destination
and you only liked me because you were bored?
i see the clock turn midnight
the honk reminds me to breathe
every car is empty
so the light slowly leaves
i start to feel more nervous
my hands begin to shake
i'm starting to feel overwhelmed
by how long healing will take
at first slowly, carefully,
one thought at a time
i repeat to myself, "you're worth loving"
the affirmations always rhyme
slowly, carefully,
i stop the car and wait
i'm looking both ways,
but i'm crashing under all the weight
i'm gripping the steering wheel
i never know what trauma will do
the vision increases with light
i'll be late when i get to you
it's raining in the city
the clock just turned to three
i'm driving by myself
as the panic sinks into me
i've been driving for hours
i can barely stay awake,
and at this point, i'm not really sure
how much more of this i can take
but i make it,
somehow, and the rain disappears
if i can drive alone,
maybe i can face all my fears

ii

in the future,
i get married today
my hair is longer than i had imagined,
and i'm writing down what i'm going to
say
"if you were to look up *vow* in the
dictionary,
i'd find you there, smiling"
i scratch out the line, though,
as i have many more memories worth
compiling
i don't know any of them yet,
but in the future, she does
so i just watch as she starts writing down
"i fell in love with you because . . ."
then i see it
in flashbacks that have yet to be told
i've never been snowboarding,
but you help me balance in the cold
and i don't really mind the freezing
as we run into a fireplace view
but then the scene shifts
there, i'm crying so hard as i lean into you
you wipe my tears then
i've never been held with so much care
you give me an empathetic look
as you kiss love letters into my hair
i've never experienced that before
your truck picks me up as it starts to rain,
and you convince me that everything i've
been waiting for
maybe wasn't in vain
then it's summers and lakes
letters and prose
the tourists leave after their visits,
but our love never goes
then it's this crazy internal battle
because i don't believe any of it to be true,
but she writes, "the best artists of our
generation
would marvel at the sight of you"
she has that already,
but for me, people just go
but today, in the future, i get married
to someone i have yet to know
and i can feel her excitement
i can see it in her mind
she genuinely believes
he was who she had to find
"serendipity" they call it
that's what she calls meeting you
i write the end of her vows:
"you are the person i wish i always knew"

iii

nobody can tell that i can't breathe,
so i scratch at the rip in my jeans
i'm hoping that, if i scratch hard enough,
i'll forget what this stupid feeling means
i can't breathe; i feel it
like a heaviness in my chest
i'm sitting in the car
desperately wishing my brain would rest
someone tries to talk to me,
but i stopped paying attention seconds ago,
and this cute little part of me
is my least favorite for people to suddenly know
they never stay long after this
i'm abandoned like a broken doll
something someone once admired
someone for whom they would never fall
i'm always in a car when it happens
silly little me
i'm just sitting here
so how bad could my anxiety really be?
then something shifts
i'm falling into a boiling pool headfirst
i'm sprinting ten miles
i'm panting from the thirst
i'm spinning in checkerboard circles
i'm scratching at the seat
he asks if i'm hungry,
but when i'm anxious, i can't eat
i'm suffocating in fresh air
i'm slamming my head into a wall
they never stay long after this
they always remember not to call
suddenly, i'm screaming in my dreams
i'm refusing any caffeine
if they knew how hard i've fought to stay,
maybe they wouldn't be so mean
i'm shaking on the floor
rough emotion stuck in air
and i HATE when this happens
he tries to touch my hair
i'm moving in a stopped car
i'm cemented to the past
and then, of course, i start crying
the frustrated tears come fast
they never stay long after this
after i've shown too much
and it has nothing to do with my body
just my mind's strong punch
it's a solo rescue mission
always me finding me
they never stay long after this
because i'm not who they wanted me to be
i put the window down
because now i really can't breathe,
and it doesn't make it any better
that i know they're about to leave
i tell him to pull over
i can't do it; i need to stop
and it always happens so suddenly
we had just been laughing in a coffee shop
he follows close behind
they always follow in the beginning
then they whisper a goodbye
while my ears are still ringing
i'm burning up from the inside
there are ants on my skin
this is what i always remember
when people ask me how i've been
heat radiates off the ground
so he puts a cold cup in my hand
he helps me get up
he balances me while i stand
and i feel it so deeply
but so suddenly i come back too
as my ears hold on to his words:
"how can i be peace for you?"

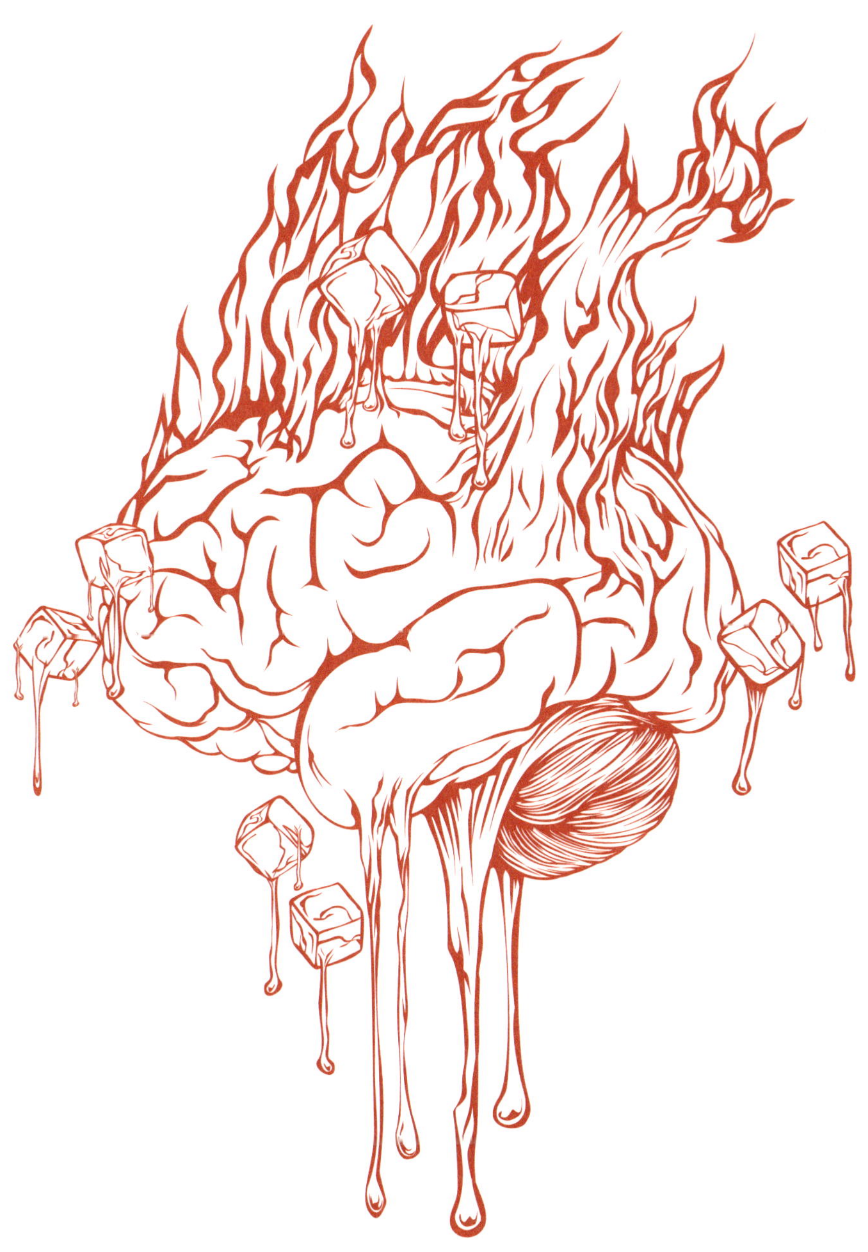

iv

i have this fear that you were it for me
that the right person does exist
that everything you are is
the reason why the poets persist
i talked to god about it
i said, “i don’t know what to do”
because everything i asked for
sounds and looks a lot like you
in that moment, everything went silent
all of heaven knew that i was afraid,
but god sat next to me and whispered,
“please trust in the plans i’ve laid”
i have this fear
that the best has passed
that when i cross the finish line,
i’ll be late and . . . last
it keeps me awake at night
i fear what i don’t know
i want someone to stay,
but i prepare for them to go
that’s what i’m afraid of—
that love does exist
but all i’ve ever known is
of what it should never consist
so i have this fear that you were it for me
because, for a split second of time,
i saw what love was
and actually believed it could be mine
i have this fear that you’re still writing
incessantly and scared,
but when it comes to speaking up,
neither of us ever dared
i have this fear that you were it for me,
and instead of saying yes,
i hesitated to love you
and made it a big mess
i said i don’t give second chances,
but honestly, that’s not true
i fear i purposefully set aside
unconditional chances just for you

v

when you learn to ride a bike,
they add training wheels to prevent your sudden falls,
but when you get older,
there's no training for when love suddenly calls
instead, there are mistakes
impostors and lies
i guess i've been the "practice" person
for a couple of "not ready to settle down yet" guys
i'm the one right before the new beginning
the interest that suddenly fades
not the girl it hurts to let go of
just one of the games in their arcades
they call me a catch to not say "safety net"
i'm the mats on the floor
i'm the foundation of an ego pedestal
until they can't use me anymore
their commitment is on a tightrope
i'm sick of being there, just below
they don't fall for me; they just fall
because they had nowhere else to go
it's a cemented truth
a heavy bag on my shoulder
some people still use training wheels for love,
even though we're older
plenty years of practice,
but i guess we never learn
i immortalize them in writing
to become just a page that they turn
a singular moment
a receipt in the trash
the memory of what once was
gone in a flash
so imagine my surprise
when someone different comes along
i say, "i've never been the right person,
just the one who's always wrong"
too much too soon
not the person with whom they try so hard to be
but when i ask why he came to the party,
he says, "there was just one person i wanted to see"
so i look behind both shoulders,
an unfortunate thing to admit,
when he says, "obviously, you—
humor me for a bit"

vi

i want you in the same way
i want a full night of sleep,
like how i want to be taken seriously
when my emotions run deep
i want you in the same way
i want to feel protected and seen
for someone to love the worst parts of me
until my slate wipes clean
i want you in the same way
i need a vacation from my mind
because the thoughts that come up about myself
are rarely, if ever, kind
i want you in the same way
i want to wake up well rested
the same way i want a relationship
that doesn't make me feel constantly tested
i want you in the same way
i want to be able to walk alone at night
without looking over shoulders
without being ready to put up a fight
i want you to understand this
i want you to really know
i want you in the same way
i want my ideal life to go
i want you to be part of it,
but i can't walk alone at night
and i want you to know that
my mind is an incredibly tired sight
i'm not well rested
i'm incredibly untrusting
if relationships were made of metal,
all of mine would be rusting
i want you in the same way
i want to try again,
but i still remember the fear that i felt
in the presence of some "loving" men
i want you in the same way
i want to forget
that some of the worst betrayals
were from people i long ago met
i want you in the same way
that i want to go home
because i'm sick of living life
just through the pictures on my phone
i want the fairy-tale ending
the romance-novel feeling
i want to be the main love interest
and not the friend who's always healing

vii

i have this recurring dream
that we end up together
i don't know if it's true,
but the alternative isn't much better
the dream starts out slowly
neither of us rushes to get up and leave
there love exists,
and in it, both of us believe
we talk about credit cards
taxes and dirty clothes
there we do the dishes together
and the time comes and goes
i serve you breakfast in the morning,
and after dinner, you make dessert
there we are together
and we've never been hurt
in the dream, i'm crying
because nobody's ever been that nice
there you treat me like sunshine warmth
instead of melting me like ice
but it's not always sunny there
the storms shake the walls
but an unlimited number of texts
and no missed calls
lightning and thunder
the power goes out
and i really don't want it to,
but there creeps in the doubt
most dreams end as nightmares
that's all i've ever known
i have this recurring dream
because that's all i've ever been shown
that we end up together
credit cards, dirty clothes
there's a fresh bouquet of flowers
and a new color for each rose
but the power goes out,
and i feel alone
because what is a spark
if not a fuse terribly blown?
it's over, i'm done
i'm trying to wake up
somebody please pour me coffee,
and i'll gulp down the cup
but the thing about dreams
is sometimes they're shared,
and i can't wake up
i didn't know you still cared

viii

"here's all the secretly written love letters,
so unfortunately, only i knew"
i ask god, "what do you mean?"
he says, "they're all about you"
he hands me this stack of paper
letters all sorts of ways
some are just a passing thought:
"in my persisting darkness, her sunshine stays"
"i'll give you a moment"
the gates suddenly close
"i saw the most beautiful girl today
i hope she believes in her beauty; i hope that she really knows"
i learn not all are paper
one is a song that keeps replaying
the same couple of chords,
like a church symphonically praying
and the notes come off the paper
they float in the air
for a second in time,
it feels like i'm really there
"he learned to play many instruments
because he couldn't find the words"
an angel sits next to me
"so he compared you to the songs of birds"
the smell of cinnamon sugar then
wafts in the breeze
he became an expert vegan baker
because you said you missed croissants and cheese
recipes fall from the pile
"it took him months to figure it out"
"i thought he didn't like me"
"you're all he's thought about"
receipts for romance novels
"do you want to go back?"
i wipe the tear from my cheek
as he hands me another stack
"i never knew that
any of this was true"
"you write about love
in the same way people think about you"
a stranger at a crosswalk
your childhood best friend
all noticed your presence
enough to have it penned
in ink, in thought
in action, in word—
all felt something
that their hearts must've heard
"you're not alone here"
"but here is heaven, no?"
"no, my darling soulmate;
here is where your own love must go"
and he wipes the tears off my face
kisses my head goodbye
"when you meet me in the future,
i will love with a library filled with all these reasons why"

ix

don't you hate pretending
that we never even kissed?
we're both sitting in a room
contemplating if the other is ever missed
and if i could, i would block you
i would never speak to you, then
i would erase every single message
if it were my choice . . . i would never see you again
and that doesn't sound too bad to me
until you enter the room,
and i think of how stupid the universe is
to have me foolishly assume
that i could just let go of it all,
forget what i wrote
while you're wearing a familiar sweater
i still remember the scent of your coat
and neither of us looks up
when we walk down the hall,
putting on the best damn performance of
"we never meant anything to each other, ever, at all"
and then the elevator opens,
and i'm stuck by your side,
and i want to look up and scream
in you, i wanted so desperately to confide
i wanted to believe you
when you ran to hold the door
i wanted to continue falling in love with you
because you convinced me not to be afraid anymore
i wanted carpool mornings,
sneaky hidden glances
i would've let you learn to love me
with an infinite number of second chances
i wanted coffee shop dates,
reading together
i wanted to be the woman
who convinced you to be better
i wanted lunches spent laughing,
complaining about the day
i wanted you to be with me for longer
than just an episode, but we got in our own way
so you press the button to my floor,
even though neither of us speaks
then you ask me how i am
i shrug; "just one of those weeks"
and we pretend that we care
in small talk, formality,
trying to be just friends
what an absolutely romantic mentality
forced to not acknowledge
forced to be kind
forced to not be the person
the other always hoped they would find
proximity is a curse
that maybe only one heart is meant to carry
but then he says, "you looked better wearing my coat"
"why don't you save it for a girl you actually care enough about to marry?"

x

he calls me beautiful,
but i hear it in your voice
how silly was i to think
my heart could make a different choice?
because when he looks into my eyes,
i see the reflection of who i could be,
but when i stared into the brown of
yours,
i think i left a piece of me
hidden between eye bags and
dark bushy brows
that part of me that writes poetry
that will someday write her vows
and his eyes are so beautiful,
but they remind me of your smile
i guess part of you is locked away
in some subconscious file
with big DO NOT OPEN letters
and extra caution signs,
they bring out the idea of us
when my card at therapy declines
and they seem so happy
so perfect, so real
so i start working extra hours
so that i don't have to feel
so the card always has money
so the file remains closed
until, just for a moment,
my heart is exposed
because when he calls me beautiful,
my definition of it has your name
when he looks into my eyes,
it never feels the same
because you've interwoven yourself
into all my best lines
like campfire smoke on a coat,
like a brick wall with its vines
how do i part from that?
when the hope still rears its head?
because when he calls me beautiful,
i wish it was something you still said

DO NOT
OPEN

xi

i was born to be a lover,
but i'm forced to be the one who got
away
because i'm excellent at inviting lust
but horrible at convincing love to stay
so i nail down a sign
to the front of my door
i was born to be a lover,
but i don't want to love anymore
call it a coping skill
or a horrible price to pay
born to be a lover
forced to be the one who got away
so i got away
lonely and alone
i slowly started to feel
like i could become my own home
eventually, the sign became a wall
stairs grew from the door
i don't want to be the one who
got away anymore
no door to knock on
the wall became a room
and i started to challenge the fact
that i only know what i assume
i was born to be a lover
that much i know
i don't want to be the one
who always has to go
so i don't; i stay
a roof and a cat
a sink, an open window
i always thought a lover would do that
one door, five
three windows, four
maybe i don't have to be
the one who got away anymore
stained glass windows,
a table made for two
i was born to be a lover,
but i forgot a lover to who
and there's one person, really,
who i could never leave
even if i wanted to,
even if i didn't believe
two stories, five
a balcony with a view
a loud boombox playing
songs i forgot i knew
born to be a lover
chosen to be the one to stay
when there's a knock on the door,
he can wait, anyway

xii

i don't mind being single,
but sometimes i get this glimpse in my head
i imagine somebody bringing me
breakfast in bed
the bedroom door opens slowly,
like he's afraid i'll suddenly wake
the smell of doughnuts fills the air
when would he have had time to bake?
he puts the tray down at the desk
with the flowers he's carefully chosen
i turn in my sleep,
and he just looks at me, frozen
like he's saving to memory the image
like he couldn't believe that it's really true
that's his "i made it" moment
he whispers, "i'm in love with you"
but he doesn't let me hear it yet
he just takes in the scene
if there was any doubt there is a heaven,
he's sure i'm what "heaven" is supposed to mean
and then my eyes slowly open
with a smile and a yawn
for a second, i panic
because i don't know where he's gone
and then, when i turn,
he's holding flowers and a tray,
he sets it down next to me
"happy birthday"
and i think i might cry
when he pulls out a little note
"i didn't want to wake you"
he takes off his coat
"i went to your favorite doughnut shop
they knew you by name
i told them you were asleep
they wished that you came"
he kisses my forehead
caresses the hair on my head
nobody has ever thought to bring me
breakfast in bed
"and i wanted to find the prettiest flowers
so i went into this floral store
when they saw my note,
they said they don't see you as much anymore

and they miss you, but they don't mind it"
i laugh with tears, wonder
as i shift in the blankets
that you must have put me under
"i didn't know you went there"
"every single birthday . . .
and when i was my own valentine,
i celebrated the same way"
"with roses and eucalyptus . . ."
i look at the bouquet
"so when i was writing this note,
i thought, what would my favorite poet say . . .
so i started with 'happy birthday'
i'm grateful you're in my life
not just in the good moments
but in the times of great strife
i can't change the past
or say what the future may hold,
but i will make it my life's mission
to love you better as we grow old
because you are a vacation
for everyone around
but also the home i want to come back to
when i arrive back in town
you are the ocean
with a love so vast
without even trying,

you make the effect of you last
so one rose for the past,
one for each valentine's day
i'm proud of you, you know
for the inspiration you convey
one for the present
one for each day of birth
an extra one to remind you
of everything you've always been worth
eucalyptus to destress
vegan doughnuts to start the day
if loving somebody could be an art,
i would make you a monet"

i don't mind being single,
but sometimes i get this glimpse in my
head
of somebody telling me that they love me
then i wake up alone in my bed

xiii

i met this girl
who holds her pain like glass,
who's gotten so used to carrying it,
she's convinced, without it, her light
won't pass
with so much to carry
and bruises on her shoulders
she saves being happy
for some day when she's older

i met this girl,
but she wouldn't fully let me inside
because when love becomes something
to seek,
you learn it's less painful to hide
because this girl, i am learning,
for a long time lived in lack,
so even when love was wrong,
she still always took them back
because something is often better
than nothing at all
but is love really love
if they're pushing you to fall?
as this girl got older,
she promised to be more
because this scarcity mindset
wasn't protecting her anymore
but the girl i had met
lingered within her still
her pain turned into a pitcher
other cups used to fill
so this girl became empty
she was never taught to say no
because when nothing ever stays,
you learn to let everything go

i met this girl
who holds her pain like it's glass,
constantly being told
that the feeling will one day pass
but one day she's so frustrated,
she screams at the wall,
starts crying so hard,
guess what she let fall?
the pieces all shatter
the shame and the guilt—
she tries to pick them up,
but they don't pair with the life she's
built
that's when i met this girl,
wounded on the floor,
and i saw her pick herself up
i don't want to carry this anymore

xiv

always the artist
never the muse
always the empath
just being used
always the epigraph
never the novel
always the clothing
never the model
always the poet
what if i want to be the poem instead
of always being the friend
who is stuck inside their head?
always giving the second chances
never seeing them return
i'm the expert they call up
when they want to learn how to yearn
always the one waiting
but showing up to an empty room
always seeing people as sunsets
when, to them, i'm just another afternoon
born to be the love interest
forced to be just the best friend
born to be the happy ending
forced to be just the end
always the writer
never being heard
always the letters
never the word
born to be the subject
forced to be behind the screen
born to understand
forced to ask, "what do you mean?"
always the heartbroken
how is that fair?
born to be thoughtful
forced to ask, "why weren't you there?"
born to be calm
forced to be anxious instead
never the slow love
just the girl they want to get into bed
always the understanding
never the understood
born to believe in love
forced to wonder how i could

xv

i don't want to go,
but you keep pushing me away
so it seems like a self-fulfilling prophecy
that nobody would ever want to stay
but it's not for the reasons you think
when you let all these hypotheses flow,
you push me away while i tell my friends,
"i still care about him, you know"
nobody will ever stay,
so you put in less effort overall
if a tree never grows,
does it ever learn how to fall?
if an ocean never meets land,
it may never need to crash,
but a wound need not be physical
to be considered such a gash
i don't want to go,
but how many chances will it take?
i pour my heart out for you
with the chance that, one day, you may
wake
from the nightmare you've created
from always being inside your head
if i could, i would save you
so you never feel that sense of dread
and i want to, but i shouldn't
because some things aren't mine to heal
but if i could, i would stay
i would remind you how to feel
because to me, love is giving,
but love need not be love to give
and maybe i do love you,
but maybe i just love to forgive
so i don't want to go,
but it's destructive for me to stay
love need not be love to give,
but love might be the reason you keep
pushing me away
why? honestly?
it's okay if i'm not the one
if that's the reason for your leaving,
well, while it lasted, i had a lot of fun
but something tells me that it's deeper
it's okay if you wanted to be more
you're unsure, not ready
you've never met a future like this before
and you're not sure who you want to be
who is that, by the way,
the version you need to be
to allow your happiness to stay?
is he kinder? more creative?
has more accolades to his name?
a less traumatic childhood?
is he the man you wish that you became?
why? to be worth loving?
what if i said i love you today?
i don't care who you could become
i think you're beautiful this way
and maybe you're not perfect
but i promise you, neither is he
the only difference you should care about:
only one of you met me
and you are so kind,
creative, and successful
believing that about yourself
shouldn't be this stressful
i don't want to go,
but you keep pushing me away,
so eventually, i just leave a note:
"for what it's worth, i loved you today"

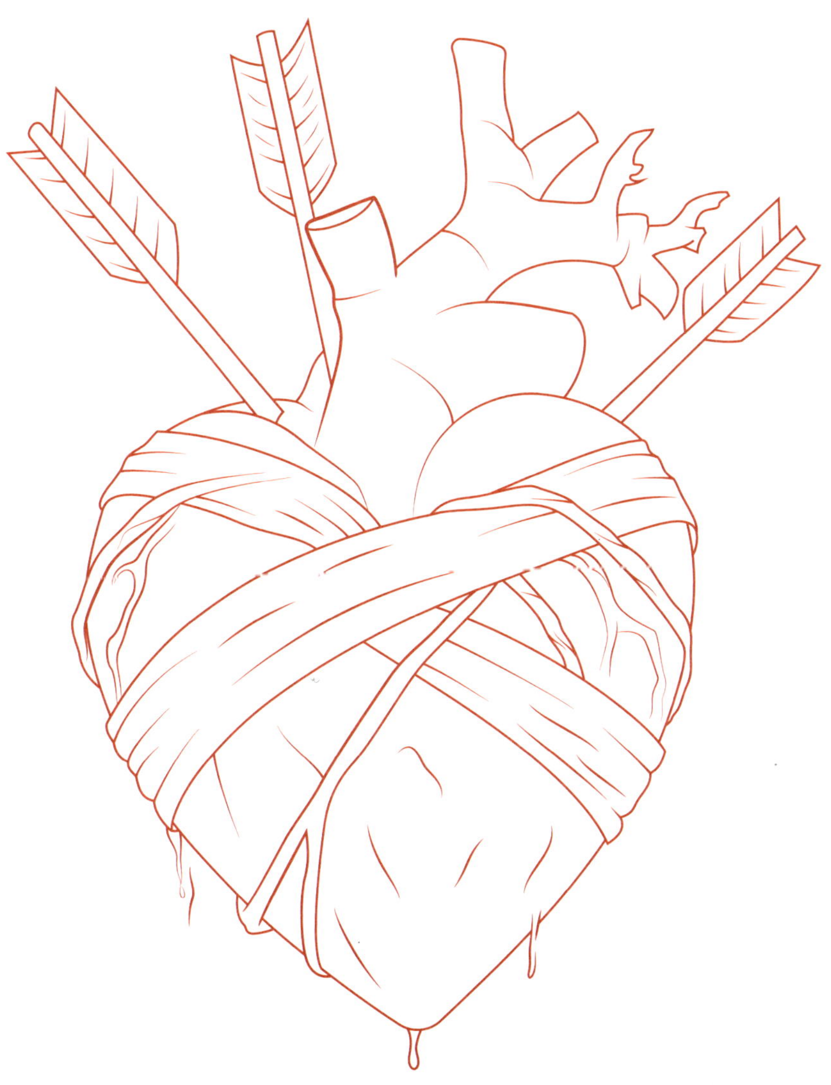

xvi

i hope today is easier
when you wake up half asleep
i hope that you forget to remember
pain you could've sworn you'd always
keep
because, *amor*, the world loves you
trees root for your growth
the poets are overflowing with
kind words for us both
for a day, which i hope is easier
for tomorrow, which will come with time
for yesterday, which was but a moment
on life's ever-rotating faceless dime
for the sides of a coin
play a hollowed, distant song
today will be easier,
and i hope that assumption isn't wrong
because it's been hard for a while
the sleeves of my sweater are so cold
every day that passes,
is another day lost, i'm bitterly told
and my feet are numb from sitting
the tips of my hands tingle with pain
there are few things more intimate than
poetry,
but every effort of mine has been in vain
disregarded, tossed aside
it's getting harder to tell what's true
how do you stay honest in a society
that rips the authenticity out of you?
i'm learning how to sew
to reclaim some of those spaces
but i'm just a needle and a thread
caught in the trendiest of places
where they don't quite like sewing
where every day is just lost
where authenticity comes
at far too great a cost
what do you do
if the person you want
wrote the essay—unrequited longing—
using you as their font?

xvii

i had to block your number
because the urge to text you wouldn't go away,
but if you asked me how i feel about you,
i would lie, "we were never that serious anyway"
while reading old text messages
while contemplating what went wrong
i had to block your number
because i liked you all along
i had kind of a rude awakening
learned that i'm not very good at letting go
i had to block your number
but your favorite birthday cake i still know
i almost learned how to make it
considered how your family could have it too
i researched dietary restrictions
even though about me . . . they pro bably never knew
i must've expressed them at some point
these emotions that most would find cute
but if i was car-ride karaoke,
you always had your radio on mute
but i was younger then,
so i believed love had a ceiling
can't give it away too fast
at least, that's how i was feeling
but then at the back of the stage,
somewhere behind a curtain,
i wished i could go back in time
to prevent you from ever hurting
to be there in the worst moments
to prevent the downward spiral
it's no surprise, really,
that even just the thought of you became viral
because to know you
is to remember you; trust me, the opposite, i've tried
i told people how great you are
i really should've lied
because now it's all different
we're just a spark that burned out
now you're just something else
that me and my therapist talk about
i look back at that time now,
how could i have felt that way?
because i've always been afraid of speaking,
but about you, only the prettiest words i could say
and they all had your crooked smile
they all had your memorable voice
i immortalized your energy
because you became my first choice
now i'm sitting on a sidewalk,
contemplating a call to make
today is your birthday
i accidentally bought your favorite cake
eventually, i'll go inside
i'll cook a warm meal
and i'll throw my heart in a cell
that nobody could ever again steal
until the cell has your number
and the phone returns to my hand
i have to block your number
because my absence, your heart still doesn't understand

Feliz Cumple

xviii

i think i made a terrible mistake
i didn't think it could be true,
but who did you tell about me,
and what did i say about you?
because it was going so perfectly
i was so happy at the start
i told my friends you're so pretty
you told your friends i'm so smart
and both of us were in it
we both wanted to be
i said my favorite thing about you
is how you treat me
because it was so beautiful
so gentle so kind
you wiped tears from my eyes,
and you kissed my anxious mind
i said i met this boy
i'm convinced he put stars in the sky
because when he looks at me,
i'm a psychological sigh
i'm fun to be around
my baggage is just a purse
i said he's better than i could've
  imagined,
and then everything got worse
and i remember the moment distinctly
i told a friend, "look who i've found"
they said you were so perfect for me
that their jaw fell to the ground
i said how well it was going
how beautifully you talk about me
how you were the book boyfriend
that i never thought in real life i'd see
my friend probably thought i was crazy
you were a guy i had just met,
but on the both of us
i would've so easily bet
because you were so funny
with the same sense of humor as i
always texting me to hang out
you struggled to say goodbye
you struggled to speak around me
swooned when i wore a dress
i wanted everything to be perfect
instead i made it such a mess
because they weren't really my friend
i learned that too late
because days later you pulled back
said that for you i shouldn't wait . . .
and i stepped into my apartment
purse fell to the ground
it suddenly felt too heavy again
when i remembered your laugh's sound
and you weren't around to wipe the tears
nobody kisses the anxious mind
i said, "look who i've found"
you heard "better you should find"
so now i don't talk about it
now i don't talk much at all
because you never know who hopes you
  tripped
when you talk about your fall

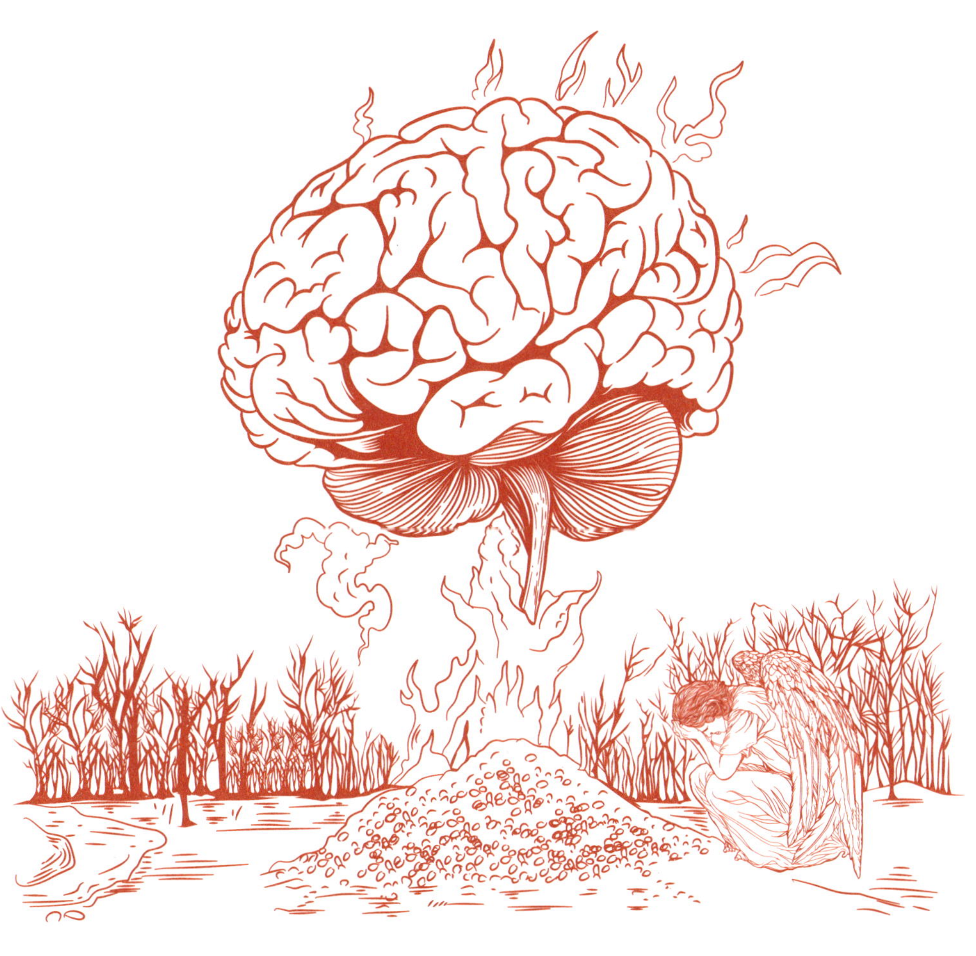

xix

i scrubbed your touch out of my hair
with shampoo that smelled like roses
i miss it sometimes now
that sadness disgustingly imposes
you said you wanted to practice braiding
for a future daughter i never knew
i liked the thought of that,
the idea of making a life with you
so we laughed as you practiced
hair full of tangles and knots
i said, "if you pull any harder,
i'm gonna start seeing dots"
and you stopped immediately,
both hands on my cheeks,
looked at me with such caution,
i remembered that look for weeks
and by weeks, i mean years
you apologized to my hair
pressed a soft kiss to my scalp
so often, i'm still there
you said, "i might need more practice"
i said, "*amor*, that's fine"
i didn't think you meant
"just needing to practice" being mine
but that day seemed so honest
like your fear went away
like you really did mean it
when you asked me if you could stay
like you were learning how to swim
and someone offered you a boat,
like you were freezing in the rain
and i came back to return your coat
as if you had never experienced it
as if you were afraid to believe it was
true
you looked at me like love was saved for
the future
but definitely not for you
and i saw that sadness,
maybe somewhere deep down,
so i said, "hey, you know what?
let's go for a drive around town"
and your light slightly flickered
your breath became uneasy
i said, "but drive a little slow
because i can get kind of queasy"
and you thought that was hilarious
you were so nervous, and for what?
for a moment, you didn't pair
"i like you" with "but . . ."
"i like you," i said
fullhearted messy hair
stuck my head back in the car
and sometimes you're still there
you don't remember it now,
but you were so nervous that day
didn't want to mess anything up
spoiler: we messed it up, anyway
but you told me about your family
your fears and your faults
and i kept those secrets hidden
in my many "made for you" vaults
where i kept that day
black shirt, no tie
how, when i came back home
i just started to cry
because you were wish fulfillment
nothing more perfect could ever be
i've been saving love for such a long
time
i didn't consider it could also be saving
itself for me

xx

you think i left because i stopped caring,
that i was looking for excuses to go
you couldn't be more wrong,
but that truth, you'll never let yourself know
because when you sit down to think about it,
it all makes sense to you
"of course i messed it up"
that feeling seems like nothing new
you write a list of all your failures,
a list of changes to make,
a list of how you can't give love,
so it would be too wrong of you to take
but you're on my list of people to pray for,
the list of people i wish to be well
you're the top of the damn list of
people for whom i easily fell
you sit down, and it makes sense to you
to be loved isn't something you choose
you think yourself undeserving of it,
but to me, you're still a muse
an aspiration to something better
a loud wish into the earth
to be soulmates in every lifetime
even if you forgot, for what it's worth
you think i left,
but every part of me stays
you write a list of all your failures
you're successful to me, anyway
despite your self-doubting,
despite your damn lists,
you've recorded every single one of your faults
i write poetry to convince you that your beauty exists
but love is not mutual destruction
love cannot change your mind
i think you're heaven on earth
you think i'm somebody else's to find
i say you're the winning lottery ticket
you say you're just a rusted penny on the floor
i say i've never seen you that way
you say you don't want to see me anymore
sometimes, some days
some months in between
then i get a text message
that i pretend not to have seen
there's a mailbox in my mind
replaying voicemails i never sent
with an infinite amount of storage
full of words you thought i never meant

xxi

we both keep pointing fingers,
as if responsibility were a dance
who messed it up when?
who deserves another chance?
do you or i move on?
do you or i accept the guilt?
who believed in it less?
whose was the foundation that was never built?
is my self-awareness
just another word for coping skill?
did i make you feel like you needed to change,
or did you just convince me that you will?
did i read into the situation,
or did you opportunistically feed me the book?
am i the one who can't get past it,
or are you still forcing me to look?
we treat our eyes like daggers
piercing with time,
pretending i never wanted to be yours,
or did you just pretend to be mine?
it's a waltz of fuzzy memory
photos dusty on the wall
did i expect too much?
or did i just want you to call?
who is most right
when everything goes wrong?
because i didn't think getting over you
would take so damn long
but it's your fault, isn't it,
unless it's somehow mine
but no, i set a boundary,
and you jumped rope with the line
a ballad of longing
a pop hit of hope
but i want to be healthy,
and toxicity is your favorite trope
a pinkie promise to be better
but no hands to hold
pointing fingers for so long,
my arm is now numb and cold
so i guess it's my fault
wrist falls to my side
i'm sorry if i didn't love you correctly,
but i really tried

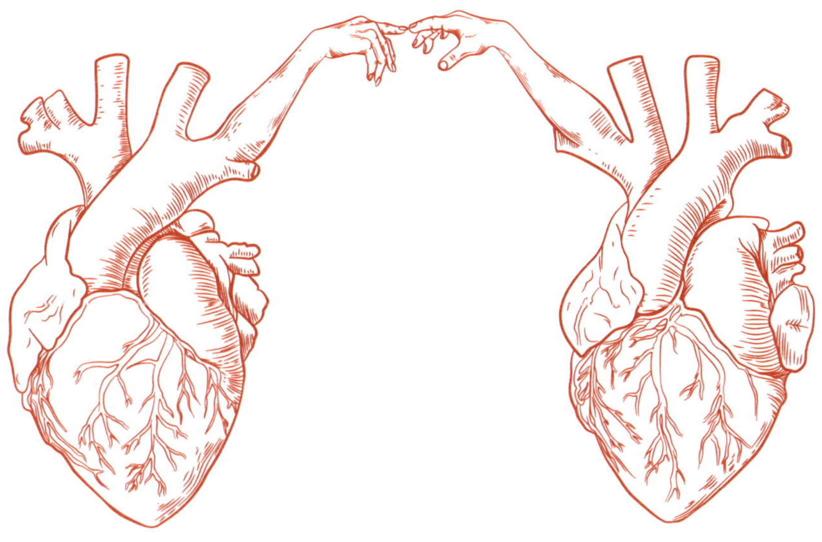

xxii

for you, i'd start running
tie up my laces and just go
i'd run and run and run
until the best version of me is the only
  one that you'll get to know
i say "you" on purpose
because, for me, that won't ever be true
i've lived through every version,
but not all will live with you
not all will be obvious
some i've hidden away
some i taught to be quiet
because i didn't like what they had to say
so some only write
some still hate to read
some look at me like i hold back
some answer that they need
maybe i do,
but not out of hate
it's because i don't want to see them
  settle
because they're afraid of being too late
afraid of love leaving
love may decide to leave
afraid of love staying
love will become what you believe
some versions of me are hidden
stuffed away in an old drawer
i couldn't bring myself to get rid of them
when i wasn't like them anymore
for you, i'd open the drawer,
no matter how painful it may be
because i want you to love and admire
every version that has ever existed of me
for you, i'd love them harder,
keep them safe and without harm
i would open the drawer slowly
so as to not cause them alarm
i'd whisper to them softly
i would let them finally speak
i would unlearn every opinion
that made me think that they were weak
because for you, i would stop running
i would learn to love the worst that i've
  been
for you, i would step back
and let some lesser version of me win
the unlovable, the annoying
the too much way too soon
the met people in the morning
and, of course, scared them away by the
  afternoon
the stupid, the impostor
the doesn't deserve to be
the wishes her heart away
for some future version, that's me
the dramatic, the confusing
the always thinks she's second best
the one who shakes from her anxiety
who works until she's forced to rest
for you, i would start walking
every version of me in hand
then i would sit, because some versions
i still can't stand

xxiii

i loved you too early
you loved me too late
so our angels sit in central park
on separate benches, forced to wait
mine left for a while
to help dry my tears
she's been with me for months
sometimes it feels like years
yours left for a while
when mine returned with roses
they say men never receive flowers
i'll give you your first, she supposes
but as she sits and smiles
and waits for your angel to walk by,
a dog rests his head on my angel's knee
she can't help but wonder why
the dog has no owner
but has a collar embroidered with time
there's some illegible name
the dog suddenly starts to whine
she leaves once to find it shelter
she leaves again to find it food
the dog won't leave her side
he wonders why anyone ever would
but the bench is the meeting place,
so she keeps forcing herself to return
she sits through every season
both the snow and summer burn
and there next to her
is that dog without a name
your bench remains empty,
and your angel never came
i call for my angel to come back
i've been without her far too long
she's a cat without her collar
the dog was never lost, all along
that's the thing about soulmates:
one can never really see
who the other person
in this life chose to be

xxiv

my room is very messy
in the house where i grew up,
but if you come in to get to know me,
there will be hot *café* in a warm cup
i can't give you more than that,
so keep your expectations low,
but the house where i grew up
is the one worth getting to know
the tile in the kitchen is stained
the blankets are all worn out
but this home here—
there's a lot to understand and learn about
i used to be afraid of the dark,
so there's glowing stars on my bedroom ceiling
mismatched notebooks that helped me carry the words
i was so heavily feeling
i used to run in cross-country races
old jerseys in my drawer
forgotten old polaroids
with people i don't talk to anymore
donated clothes that used to be my favorite
a passed-down guitar hangs on my wall
my house is very imperfect
but very loved, despite it all
some of the paint is a little different
many things about it aren't the same
but baby pictures rest on the furniture
here, i'm called only by my middle name
i grew up here, i cried here
for a long time, here i couldn't be
but this messy house
is the reason i am me
the doors don't really close right,
and privacy is hard to find
the shower might be a little clogged
but this house is home, when it comes to mind
there are pots and pans in the oven
there are our handprints in the cement
my hands have gotten much bigger since then
i've written more letters i never sent
this messy house of mine?
i used to be ashamed
the floors are all scratched up
my insecurities are all framed
but here exists a part of me
i struggle to feel i truly know
i've forgotten so much about me
here is where my childhood self feels safe enough to go
because her hands rest on the cement
her laugh is in the walls
this messy house of mine
still answers my heart when it calls
it is not a mansion
it is not perfectly made
the colors on the blankets
i've watched them all fade
but if you come in and you love it,
if it too makes you feel at home,
you'll understand that perfection
cannot hold the entirety of beauty alone

SUMMER *(now)*

i

i bought a one-way ticket
and packed in my bag only a dream
i said i felt excited to go
not everything is always how we make
  it seem
the whole family stood there
hugs and kisses and goodbyes
and i tried to say it wasn't hard,
but i've never been good at telling lies
the two-minute walk to airport security
held tears like they were hands
this is the kind of sacrifice
that not everybody understands
i sit at the airport gate
all our locations still say we're seconds
  away
part of me begs to turn back
part of me wonders what my life would
  be like if i were to stay
so i dial my mom's number
"hi, mama, i'm sitting at the gate"
"*bueno, mija, que te vaya bien*
we don't want you to be late"
the back of my throat burns
with a plea to want less
to want closer, more convenient,
a life i could more easily guess
but how do you say no
to changing your life?
to the ability to raise the ceiling,
to being able to choose if you're
  someone's wife?
to careers and access
to titles and time
how many poems go unappreciated
just because their translation doesn't
  rhyme?
it's a one-way ticket,
and there's no looking back
as soon as i get on that plane,
my life is on an entirely different track
some colleges become diplomas,
doctorates some day
as soon as we take off,
my kids will be raised in an entirely
  different way
i bought a one-way ticket
with money i had saved
with the sacrifices that made it so
this path for me had been paved
and as i walked upon it,
the road narrowed to a slit
i'm on a single-file line
where we move forward bit by bit
and i look back briefly
so fast, i almost get stuck
the only reason i made it this far
must be from sheer dumb luck
i bought a one-way ticket,
and when i sat in the seat,
part of me was excited,
but being apart means i'm incomplete
so i held myself steady
to find balance with the something new
i opened up my bag to grab a sweater,
but the dream i made was supposed to
  include you

ii

i never wanted to be "famous"
i just wanted to be known well by you,
so i put my diary online,
and the rest of the world fell for you too
for a girl who hates public displays of affection,
i might have had a change of heart
because all these declarations of appreciation
are just confessions i call "art"
the audience doesn't even know the full story,
just the excerpts i've fictionalized to rhyme
and if i put them all together,
a very complicated story they would find
"but it is quite the story,"
i hear my friends say
we're sipping wine over a pizza
"and did you talk to him today?"
everyone knows the answer
"damn, so it'll be a good poem, then!"
and if you look hard enough,
there are pieces of you in all my fictional men
good thing i don't write novels
well, not yet; too soon, i guess
because every new story
would be us absent of our mess
i walk into my house now
my back against the door
keys hung, lights on
i don't know if i can write about this anymore
i bite the nail of my thumb
the sun is starting to set
you would have made me a poet
even if i had never written yet
deep breath in
i type it all out
i hate pda, but
you're all i can write about
it's getting harder to keep secret
especially to myself too,
because he looks at me
while i am still thinking of you
i'm sorry, i'm sorry,
i'm sorry a million times
because you are so much more to me
than just endless letters and rhymes
i unlock the door then
i get in the car and drive
writing has been the only thing
that makes me feel like i will survive
then there was more,
daylight savings and hope
i started reading again
with stress, i better cope
i look at the rearview mirror
there's so much i left behind
eyes back to the road now
because better, i was meant to find
i'm glad to have moved closer
you're not that far away
car parked, door closed
"i have something i've been needing to say . . .
i never wanted to be 'famous'
i just wanted to be known well by you
and there's a lot that i have learned
so maybe this mindset is kind of new
but at one point, i knew you,
and it was enough for me to want to try
to be someone better"
my eyes look to the sky
for a girl who hates public displays of affection,
my affection for you, i need not feign
especially when i look up from my writing
and notice you're on the same train

iii

when i moved back home,
i thought that we were done
there was nothing left to say
i was sad that you hadn't been the one

maybe it had just been convenient
same place, same job
if love was a door,
maybe you had just turned the wrong
knob

it happens, i told myself
mistakes are bound to occur
i threw myself into writing
because happier endings i tend to prefer

but as i sat on the train
where the coast faces west,
i heard a laugh
that i once considered to be the best

and i turned, and there you were,
frozen like a thought
my voice in my throat
but no words to be caught

brown eyes, lighter hair,
a sweatshirt from a new school
if i believed in coincidences,
i'd be a damn fool

i turned, body forward
into san francisco we go
we're underneath the tunnel
that i once imagined you would know

you aren't supposed to be here
you were supposed to stay east
i thought you would've mentioned
a change of plans, at least
but i guess i didn't, either,
when i changed my mind
i hear my name called behind me,
so i turn; your eyes are still kind

iv

i didn't think i'd see you
after we said our goodbyes
we sat on your floor
deciphering miscommunications, lies
i'm surprised you came back
last i heard, you had new dreams
you said you'd never cut your hair
a lot has changed now, it seems

you look well rested
before, you struggled to stay asleep
i haven't brought myself to toss away
all these facts about you that i still keep

"hey, what a surprise,"
i hear myself say
"i didn't think i'd run into you"
ever, not just today

"yeah, i guess i could say
the same thing about you,
but i do kind of live here—
wait, do you live here now too?"

a brief moment, just a pause
how will the "yes" be taken?
part of me misses sleeping
in the same bad we used to wake in

"yeah, just moved
into an apartment downtown
now i understand why you missed it"
i feel my smile become a frown

"oh nice, great,
has school started?" he points
i drop my eyes to my sweater
i feel weakness in my joints

"uh, yes, a couple of weeks ago
everybody is really nice"
i never thought i'd meet you once,
let alone meet you twice

v

to me, you're perfect,
but the thing about perfect is, it's
insecure
the meaning keeps changing,
so you wait for the next visitor
to tell you that you're perfect,
but you feel that it's a lie
someone so perfect
wouldn't ever need to try
and you wake up in the morning,
the same routine done in vain
a day to keep pretending
"the impostor goes insane"
to me, you're perfect,
but at home you think you're dumb
you rest an ice pack on your heart
because it's better off being numb
the car ignition plays
a list of all my lies
i tell you that you're perfect,
the lowest low of all your highs
and as you're driving, you wipe a tear,
another, maybe three
you keep fucking crying
that perfect? you don't see
so you park the car and sit there
everybody else can be just fine,
but you open the trunk and put all your
worries
on a textbook *dsm* shrine
"perfect" isn't in there;
none of the answers that you need
how do you climb a tree
that you think is still just a seed?
i think you're perfect
you think that i'm wrong
you think it isn't about you
when i write another song
but then it starts playing,
and the words kind of make sense
you open all the windows,
waiting for the hate to commence
airing out the illusion
you think you could never be
i wish that all your mirrors
were created by me
but i can never capture it,
the full encapsulation
there are ink marks on my arms
from all this artistic frustration

STAY

vi

the train stops early
halfway to our two houses,
we're both hesitant to find out
if there await unknown spouses

"well, it was nice seeing you"
deep breath, just make it to the door
as i start to exit, he says my name again
just like he used to say it before

dangerous territory
because the same feeling persists
he is one of the few people
i still don't believe really exists

"would you like to grab coffee?
actually, no, i meant tea . . .
i'd love to keep talking—
that is, if you don't mind talking to me"

"sure," i find myself saying
"sure? we don't have to, if you don't
   want"
this is the kind of crossroads
that regrets tend to haunt

but we order two teas
i haven't had coffee in years
he's the embodiment of my reflection
as we sit there, two mirrors

vii

if i were to call you beautiful,
beauty would need a new definition
because god put you together
to make gorgeous have a more ethereal
  rendition
you're beautiful
in the way that your energy floats,
like it's freezing outside
and you brought infinite coats
so that everyone would feel comfortable,
you're beautiful in how you speak
the first time you talked to me,
i replayed it in my head for a week
if i were to call you beautiful,
you'd shake your head and blush
while i'd hold on to the table
as the butterflies started to rush
beautiful in how you listen
to an endless stream of thoughts
i compared the light in your eyes to those
  found on ceilings,
but stars don't share the same watts
you're beautiful in the way
poets string together words,
like every single part of you
was placed into perfection by a pair of
  hummingbirds
you're beautiful
so much so, i need to look away
because if i look into your eyes,
i forget what i was gonna say
the sky blues at your absence,
but even when it cries,
the rainbows form to help
guide us to one day realize
that there's art in sadness
i'm sad that you don't know
that i think you're so beautiful,
and that made me want to let you go
because beauty kept secret
is like standing in the shade
you never know the sun's warmth
if, in its absence, you always stayed
and i should've stayed,
even if i'd stood there in awe
with no words to be formed,
i couldn't find a single flaw
because you're beautiful today,
beautiful tomorrow
i went and begged the sun
for some of its beauty to borrow
instead, she showed me your smile,
then took a picture of mine
handed me a pen
and i described you in every line

viii

i never got over it
i just pretended to get through
because how does one get over
the regret of losing you?
my desk drawer is obsessed
with all the futures that could have been
to me, you were heaven
heaven should never be tainted by sin
you are perfect, polished
a pleasure to know
i never could've compared
to the place where angels go
you're well-spoken
well-mannered, worth every reason to fall,
but if you'd never met me,
it wouldn't have mattered at all
if words were made of pennies,
you'd create lotteries that rhyme
i made myself a millionaire
because it wasn't the right time
but i wish it had been,
and i hold those thoughts like a prayer
to say or not to say,
a better man wouldn't dare
but i confess,
before i know if i should:
"i never got over you
honestly, i don't think i ever could
i loved you immediately;
it was a dopamine rush
never felt that way before
with any other crush
because i loved you
before love had time to fall
i loved you even when i said
i didn't like you much at all
i loved you, i did
sometimes i still do
when i compare every first date
to that first one i had with you
i loved you, i did
to call it something else is cruel
when you read over essays
after i confided how i wanted to go back to school
so i started baking,
making myself better
i loved you so much,
i used it as a new standard-setter
because if i could love you,
that love with me remains
and i'm really hoping this is the part
where you mention these were just growing pains
that i'll understand when i'm older,
when i'm somehow less naive
how can you still love someone
when you know they're supposed to leave?
don't leave, i loved you
don't leave, please stay
don't leave because that love
won't leave my heart anyway
don't leave, i didn't say it
don't leave, i wish i had
don't leave because i know the future,
and without you, it's pretty sad
don't leave, i mean it
don't leave or let me go
leave if you must,
but i need you to know
that i think part of me will always love you
but if you were never to return,
what a hell of a lesson
the loss of you was to learn"

ix

i thought it didn't matter
when i got on that plane
numbness was a sensation
that i didn't need to feign

i put off heartbreak
because it didn't fit in my schedule
until it washed over me,
until my diary was illegible

and you decide now it's right,
that the time works best for you
you didn't even consider
what i could be going through

now it's all perfect,
everything bad is gone
you're listing out pros
when i see one huge con

what if it didn't work out
because it was never meant to be
who are you in love with?
because it didn't feel like you loved me

when i moved back home,
i thought it'd be a clean break
now you're here confessing,
but really, for whose sake?

you never said anything
i guess, neither did i
how many allergies did i pretend to have
just for an excuse to be able to cry?

x

i hope it gets better
that you don't have to overshare
that you don't second-guess
if they do or don't care
they do care, i promise
you can take it very slow
you don't have to rush into anything
i'll pick you up if you want to go
i know it gets better,
but some days it'll feel like hell
you'll be on a plane hyperventilating,
and nobody will be able to tell
i will, i promise,
and one day, when you ask me why,
i won't tell you the whole story
just the parts that don't make me cry
i can't say certain things without crying
it gets better, but some days it's the same
i hope one day you believe me
when i say you weren't to blame
it wasn't your fault
that guilt that you carry,
you don't have to hold it
it isn't yours to bury
i don't just hope it gets better
i hope it disappears
that you'll feel safe with somebody,
that you'll share all your fears
the irrational, the crazy,
the actually makes a lot of sense
when you hold trauma in your body,
all your muscles tense
i hope there's a day
when life feels like a massage
when you're getting into your dream car
when there's a big garage
a big house, a big yard
a big life to live
i hope you get back the totality
of all the love you give
tenfold, twenty-fold,
fifty-fold today
that's all i need to know—
that it'll be okay

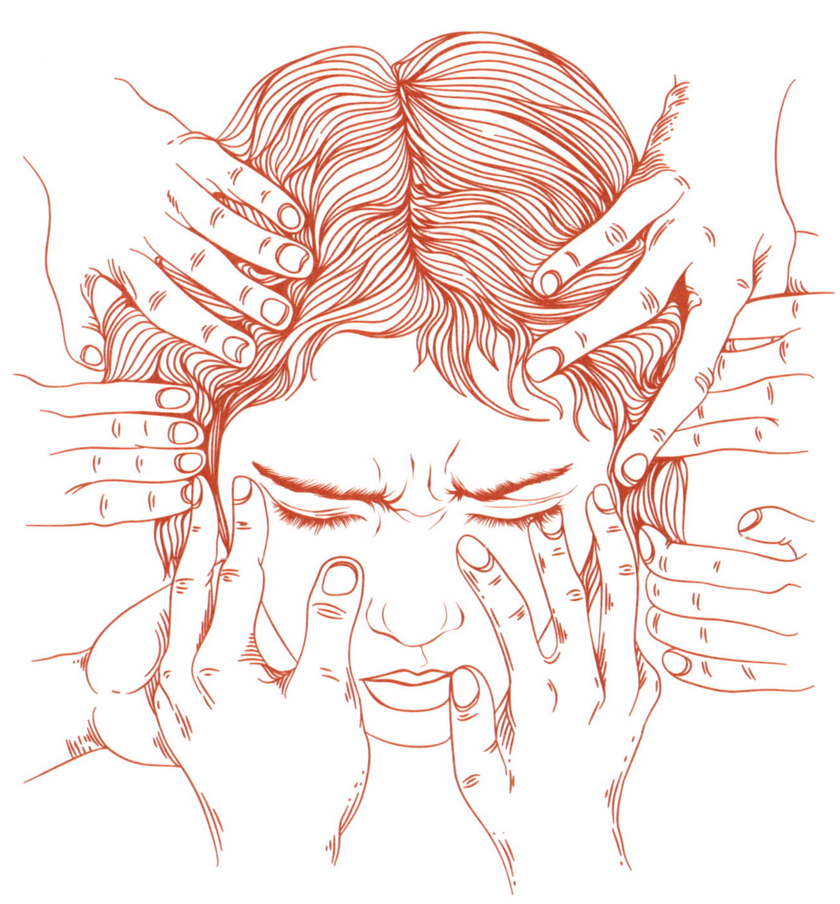

xi

she starts to get up,
starts taking steps back
just how many details
does her idea of me lack?

because i love her
more obvious, i couldn't be,
but i never got over the fact
that she's not supposed to end up with
me

"you can't be serious"
she's clearly upset
i shouldn't have said anything
her soulmate, she should've met

but i'm selfish and stubborn,
and she is the sun
how do you convince someone else's
soulmate
that you're better than their real one?

so i take out notebooks,
receipts, my phone
what do they all have in common?
they contain the love i wish i'd shown

so she starts reading,
first angry then in awe
this is the kind of communication
that in past relationships, we never saw

the dots start connecting,
each action held a phrase
if love was paid in salaries,
this was an overdue raise

i never thought i'd get the chance
to rewrite every lie,
every omission i'd been documenting,
even before we said goodbye
but here it all is,
the secret never told
we could've been together
i watch every poem unfold

xii

the day that you moved,
i set my computer to eastern time
you were always in the future,
so i waited for my phone to chime
with how you were doing
or the weather that day
if it was cold or extra sunny,
i made a note of what you would say
you hated the winter,
always missed the sun
it was snowing where you were,
and you couldn't wait for it to be done
you said you missed california,
how the winter was summer in disguise
you said you missed a lot of things,
but facetime couldn't decipher that in
your eyes
so i asked, "what do you miss?"
hoping, at some point, i would be listed
the day that you moved,
a part of me somewhere else existed
and you said some pastries,
some coffee shops, some views,
you said you missed a lot of things,
some you hated to lose
like some friends, some comfort,
some downtown familiar roads
i sat there attentively,
wondering what it all encodes
the day that you moved,
it started to rain
you asked about my weather
i secretly wished i was on a plane
you asked what i missed,
and i said the snow
you said the only time you liked it
was when, to my house, you could still
go
the day that you moved,
california i missed
though my flight was headed west,
that sun i hadn't kissed
and as i was thinking, you interrupted
to add something new
you said you missed a lot of things,
none compared to how much i've missed
you

xiii

you never forget when you truly love
someone
you just keep pushing it aside,
hoping and begging
the sentiment will abide

will see itself out
when the room grows quiet
i told myself i didn't love you
at no point did i buy it

over and over,
the conviction would lack
i would avoid the thought of you
because i hoped you'd come back

your presence, your aura,
your cleverness, your drive
when we were together
i felt more alive

because you make life romantic,
like everything is a movie scene
i've read a lot of books
none compare to what i've seen

i loved you with patience
i loved you with fear
i loved you in words
i thought you'd never hear

you hand me a notebook
i hand you three back
we're standing over feelings
we were made to believe we should lack

it's time to be honest
i never let it go
the thing about secrets,
they become truths we all know

xiv

there's an entry in my diary
where my future husband is named
a fictitious character
with characteristics that could be framed

that could make out a person
a photograph, someday
there's an entry i had written
that i'm giving to you today

i heard wishes come true
when they're named and dated
imagine my surprise
when it was your name that was stated

brown hair, brown eyes
witty, kind of shy
imagine my surprise
when you were word for word the same
guy

and the entry is from fifteen years ago
your name followed me where i went
popped up like an internet router
connection
when my sanity had been spent

the idea of you wasn't imagined
it was transcribed from something more
angels whispered in my ear what you
were like
when i couldn't believe in you anymore

and word for word the same meeting
word for word the unfortunate lie
i didn't just write a hello
for some stupid reason, i wrote in a
goodbye

so i keep getting déjà vu
when i see the way you act
the dream wasn't some perfect person
it was you, word for word, exact

xv

with you, i feel safe
i feel like i can breathe,
like it wouldn't ever be too much
to admit how much help i really need
like i can be honest about everything,
not just the parts of me that people like
like when you tell me i'm beautiful,
i don't internally say, "psych!"
with you, i feel beautiful
i think beauty persists
because i see it in your eyes
i believe that love exists
with you i feel safe
on a plane, in a car
you're the first person i look for
you could be a shooting star
because when i see you, wishes are granted
wishes can come true,
and you have no idea
how long i've been wishing for you
with you i feel important,
like everything that i say
is worth being known
is appreciated every day
like art can be made
just for art's sake
like you are the theme
of every love poem i make
with you i feel safe,
so i keep letting myself grow
you have no idea how
many versions of me i've been waiting for
  you to know
until i felt safe
and wanted and not like a bore
with you i don't want to be
casual anymore

xvi

if you knew how i feel about you,
your poems would write themselves
in awe of the masterpieces
that somehow left their shelves

because poetry is, of course, poetic
but a reflection of the poet they describe,
you are the dream lover
my angels begged god to transcribe

and, of course, words hold meaning,
but meanings changed when i met you
brown hair, brown eyes
now my favorite view

anxiety was my worst enemy
for the way that it harmed
so anytime i saw you were upset,
with peace, i came armed

i want to be peace for you
i want to be ease
i want to be around
will you let me now, please?

words hold meaning,
but words don't know the weight of your hand
the feel of your breathing on my chest
they'll never understand

and i tried to explain
that it all meant something more,
but words are just words
if they've never been in love before

if you knew how i felt about you,
everything would change
because if you asked me to come over,
my whole life, i'd rearrange

intentionally, thoughtfully,
drawers would be cleared
on the train, i wished to meet my future wife,
and guess who appeared?

xvii

often when you meet someone,
you classify them as one of two
someone you met once,
and then there's somebody like you,
who meeting once feels like
meeting several times before,
like looking into a reflection
of someone you thought you'd never find
anymore
and that makes everything so exciting,
that time doesn't feel very real,
so you find it kind of alarming
how one person could make you feel
suddenly, one of two things happens
you fall in love, or you don't
because who doesn't love seeing
themselves
in a way that many can't, or simply
won't?
and so when i met you,
i met a glimpse of who i could be
there was you, yes,
but also the realization there exists a
better me
the blissfully ignorant part of me
assumed that this was the best
all of who i am
was just the next grade of a test
and then you come in,
and you're not perfect, but to me you are
you come in and make all those
impossible dreams
seem like maybe they're not so far
but the one thing i feared
was the sudden relief to be complacent
if i met someone so great,
what would the rest of my life be if not
just to you, adjacent?
and so those dreams seated on clouds of
doubt,
suddenly puffed out their chest,
reminded me of their presence
until i forgot how to rest
you said once that meeting me
put you in a sugar coma of pleasure
the thought of you, to me,
was a candy shop where i, for once,
allowed myself not to measure
so though i had been writing,
my writing transformed
like every major epiphany i ever had,
suddenly, to my mind, swarmed
because, at that moment,
the floodgates of hope
busted at the seams
so i went back to therapy to cope
i realized love is not always magnificent
my love for you, on paper, was ordinary
as we sit now overlooking the city,
i offer my hand and one last thought to
carry
you are not perfect,
but you never had to be
to pull some of the most beautiful poetry
so effortlessly out of me

Thank you to all the wonderful artists who helped bring the poems to life:

- Creative Director: Martín Martínez
- Cover: Nishani Thilakarathne
- Poetry Artists, in order of contributions: Alis Wibowo, Surender Kumar, Jh Erfan, juwelz

The words *thank you* would never be able to fully encompass the amount of gratitude I have for this book and all of you. Writing has healed me in ways I didn't even think were possible. Love is complicated and messy and extraordinary in the ways it is expressed, and honestly, the inspiration for this book I never would have guessed. Prior to finding poetry, I struggled to put my emotions into words; now I see emotions as stories waiting to be told. Paragraphs are dance partners, indentations hold space for more, and commas are abundant, warm hands to hold. The most mundane can be poetic if you let it be. You are already poetry to me.

In order to understand one's emotions, one must verbalize them. My friends, family, and mentors were instrumental in helping me find my voice. So now I stand here and clear it, shaky notebook paper in hand, telling you about all the ways in which they helped me understand. I am thankful for the heartbreak and thankful for the love, but most of all I'm thankful for the ways in which I fell and still chose to look above. To the memories, to the places, to the things I left behind, I hope each of you read these pages and some long-forgotten hidden part of yourself you take a moment to find.

To my parents, *gracias por su apoyo. A mi hermano, gracias por ayudarme en la creación de este libro.* To James for representing me as a wonderful literary agent. To Danys for all her insightful edits. To so many who believed in me even when I didn't believe in myself.

Writing a book is no easy feat, and in the same way that healing cannot be done in a day, this collection was inspired by a variety of situations and people over the span of multiple years. To those inspirations, thank you for helping me grow.

Finally, to baby Celia: I'm so proud of you.

¡SI SE PUDO!

About the Author

Celia Martínez is a Mexican American bilingual poet and hopeful romantic. She began posting her work on TikTok in 2021 and quickly amassed a following of more than three million on TikTok and one million on Instagram. Martínez graduated from Yale University with a BS in molecular, cellular, and developmental biology and is a proud *mujer* in STEM.

You can follow Celia Martínez on Instagram and TikTok.

@diaryofaromantica

@powerhouseofthecel